Too Cool To LOVE

TERRELL MACLIN

IMELIFE.COM

www.affordablebookpublishing.org

Copyright © 2022 Terrell Maclin
Photos by Tim Alexander

ISBN: 978-0-578-99216-7

Library of Congress Control Number: 2022904946

All rights reserved. No part of this publication may be reproduced, distributed, or transmitted in any form or by any means, including photocopying, recording, or other electronic or mechanical methods, without the prior written permission of the publisher, except in the case of brief quotations embodied in critical reviews and certain other noncommercial uses permitted by copyright law. For permission requests, contact affordablebookteam@gmail.com.

CONTENTS

Acknowledgements *I*
Introduction *VI*
1 Confession *1*
2 What Is Love? *10*
3 Truth *22*
4 Too Cool To LOVE *35*
5 The Tool Box *57*
6 Life's Too Short *72*
7 The Trophy Life *80*
8 WTF *95*
9 Social Serpents *109*
10 R. A. P. E. *121*
11 State of Emergency *138*
12 Health Check *165*
13 Purge *170*
14 No Days Off *198*
15 ObeyLOVE *210*
~ NOTES AND JOURNAL SECTION

Before you begin to read this book, please scan the QR code. The contents of it will help you to access the Too Cool To LOVE platform including the exclusive soundtrack, along with the entire Spotify playlist for the book.

The QR is a live (digital) link that will consistently be updated to provide other helpful resources along your journey, including live coaching sessions, entertainment, special offers, and more..

The goal is to ensure that you are learning and growth experiences will continue long after you finish reading or listening to the Too Cool To LOVE E-book.

Using the QR code is optional, but scanning it is highly recommended (GO DIGI).

Acknowledgements

I'd like to express my heartfelt gratitude to the incredible individuals who have played instrumental roles in shaping this book and my life. Without your support, guidance, and inspiration, "Too Cool To LOVE" would not have been possible. Each of you has left an indelible mark on my journey, and I am forever grateful for your contributions.

First and foremost, my heartfelt appreciation goes to my mother, Constance Maclin, and my sisters, Cherria and Cheryl Maclin. You have exemplified the strength and resilience of empowered women, showing me the importance of standing up for what's right and embracing respect. Your unwavering support has been the cornerstone of my inspiration. And for my brothers Andre, James and Mario, thanks for loving and protecting me, shielding me from the violent part of our upbringing. Without big brothers like you, my level of peace would not be as resilient. To my nieces and nephews, the legacy and billions of dollars I plan to leave behind are for you. Take them and rise up to be a shining example, and an extension of our lineage. To Frances Maclin, thanks for being my mother from another, yet giving me your all as if I were your very own. Without question, you shaped other important aspects of me. And to my Dad Charles Curtis Maclin, even though you are gone from earth, long lives the King in me.

Too Cool To LOVE

To my dear friend and business colleague, Robert Richardson, thank you for being a driving force, not only in my life, but as part of this project. You turned my initial doubts into a burning desire to share the truth, providing unyielding encouragement and professionalism throughout. As we continue to navigate the challenges of life together, your grace is always a guiding light.

I extend my deep thanks and appreciation to Lawrence Bailey for the initial financial investment in iMe Corp and the golden opportunities you've provided me over the years. Our friendship and brotherhood have had some bumps in the road, but that is what made us stronger, and I look forward to the next chapters of growth.

To my mentor, Jonathan Webb, and his lovely wife Liz, your guidance and belief in my gift are monumental. You have also been a constant reminder of what other good men look like. Even though you have moved on to handle your heavenly business, your presence, wisdom and knowledge remain with me. I intend to do exactly what you knew I would, and this book is only the beginning.

A special shoutout to Mr. John Stenson, ESQ, not just as my attorney but as a dear friend and a shining example of goodness. Getting to know you over the past decade has been a source of inspiration, and your sensibility and impeccable fashion sense have been motivating factors on my journey. You also keenly represent the awesome little brother I never had.

Too Cool To LOVE

I'm deeply grateful to Kaysha King, editor-in-chief at Kaysha King LLC, whose unwavering support allowed me to express myself authentically. Kaysha, your insistence on addressing important topics pushed me to explore uncharted territories. Your strength, personality, and grace have fueled me during moments of self-doubt. Your patience, encouragement, and support are priceless.

Chico Bennett, J1 (John Webb), and Flip (Emmanuel Fipps), you are my innovative Rocks of Gibraltar. Your talents and inspiration have shaped my history and ongoing creative works, and I'm humbled by the hours we've dedicated to our shared body of work. I'm eager to share a Grammy or other such accolades with you all.

Shirley Strawberry, your tough love during a pivotal moment was a turning point I'll never forget. Your candid advice, given with love, was exactly what I needed. I thank you for helping me review and revisit my steps when I needed it most.

Tim Alexander (TAKA Productions), you've been my go-to for photographs and images for a remarkable twenty-five years. Your ability to capture my brand and create iconic pieces, including the *Too Cool To LOVE* book cover, is deeply appreciated. Your knowledge and expertise have been invaluable.

KerryAnn Morrison, my sister from another mister. I am thrilled you have connected with my family and friends, and have opened up to receive my brotherly love, which has helped us all to experience an authentic bond. Alongside that, thank you for also being the who, what, why and how for the iMeLife brand. Your focused determination is second to none (appreciate ya!).

Your design and printing expertise have also elevated the iMe and Too Cool To LOVE brands, and I'm immensely grateful.

I must acknowledge the one and only Oprah Winfrey. The trepidation I felt while writing this book was reminiscent of the day I appeared on your show. Both moments were fueled by a shared theme: women, broken relationships, and the pain caused by men. It was a dark place that I couldn't shy away from. Purging those emotions and truths changed my perspective, and purpose. Your intuition caused you to suggest that I had a broader role to play, related to the Sister I'm Sorry episode we shared in. Your notion and expectations of me helped to put me in the driver's seat, for the Too Cool To LOVE journey. And here we are.

Mr. Steve Harvey, your presence as a friend of the family has been inspirational. Seeing a fellow "homeboy" from the hood rise to your level motivates me. And even though you famously teased me when I was seventeen ("Sad About It"), your body of work speaks for itself, and it continues to propel me daily. Regardless of the miles that are often between us, you have always made me feel special.

P. Miller (Master P), you know what it is. I acknowledge you because you gave me a few opportunities to realize my creative aspirations when no one else would. You also gave me some

Too Cool To LOVE

of the best advice ("stop having paralysis by analysis"), and get in the game. Well, here I am. And yes, I am still going to pay you that 100k consulting fee that we always joke about.

Family is important, and most of you here are tried and true family to me. That said, a special shout out goes to the Thacker family. Shawn, you, Pops and the entire Thacker clan have been my family away from home ever since we met 30 years ago. I love you bro, and appreciate the soul tie kind ship.

And last but certainly not least, Kyoko Love. Your beautiful music and profound chords of wisdom and knowledge have added significant depth to my life's piano. I thank you for singing such beautiful high notes. I will forever be inspired by you.

This book and my journey have been more transparent than I initially planned, and they took longer than expected, resulting in me neglecting friends and family along the way. To all those who've carried heavy instruments or played in the band during my life journey, I am deeply indebted to you.

Today, as I rise from the ashes and building blocks of yesterday's experiences and setbacks, I stand with confidence, knowledge, power, and conviction. It's time for me to step into my destiny, a moment that wouldn't have been possible without each and every one of you. Thank you for being a part of my life, helping me become stronger, focused, poised, and ready to embrace what lies ahead.

Introduction

Welcome to the *Too Cool To LOVE* experience. This book will not only help you identify individuals that are masking dysfunction and inappropriate behaviors in your life, but it will also serve as a study guide that provides the tools and the necessary building blocks for self-love and self-empowerment.

Prepare yourself for a journey that delves deep into the intricate world of relationships and dating in today's instant-gratification via social media environment. In these unprecedented times and culture, we find ourselves at a pivotal juncture where the bedrock principles of love, truth, honor and respect are lost, and demand our attention. These fundamental elements were, and should always be, a part of the compass that guides us toward true love and fulfillment, therefore, their reclamation is paramount.

As you immerse yourself in these pages, I am hopeful that the lessons serve as a bridge, intertwining the moral threads woven throughout past dating and relationship cultures, while offering fresh perspectives for those seeking love in the present day.

Brace yourself, because this journey might occasionally lead you into discomfort. The truths revealed herein will unveil the secrets that reside in the depths of your heart and soul. I implore you to please not shrink away from this process. Allow this profound exploration to unfold, for it's only by illuminating the darkest corners of our being that genuine healing can truly commence. The reward for enduring this transformation will be the radiant glow of successful relationships, a renewed mind, a fortified heart, and an elevated overall disposition.

With the arrival of 2024, a new odyssey unfolds. I set forth on a quest not only to convey a pivotal message about relationships but to sculpt a renaissance for love, breathing fresh vitality into its visage, infusing it with a potent social resonance.

The impetus behind my endeavor to pen this book and share these invaluable relationship lessons emanates from the very essence of my being. My top 5 reasons for providing the Too Cool To LOVE study guide are as follows:

- 1. Championing Honor and Integrity: I am resolute in my belief that the crucial dialogue surrounding honor and integrity in relationships has too often been sidelined, and the time has come for us to illuminate these principles with unwavering clarity.

- 2. Avoiding Disappointment: I firmly believe that the heartaches and disappointments we encounter in relationships can be mitigated with the wisdom shared within these Too Cool To LOVE pages.

- 3. Men as Mentors: I firmly believe that men hold a profound duty to lead and uplift one another in the relentless pursuit to establish truth and the embodiment of honor.

- 4. Empowering Women: The winds of change have swept across the realm of relationships, and women have profoundly established their voice. It's a crucial time, and I am compelled to contribute to this transformative period.

- 5. Truth and Love as Catalysts: Without a doubt, I recognize that truth and love form the bedrock, essential for conquering every challenge. With this understanding, I am deeply honored to serve as a catalyst on this evolutionary journey.

So, my dearest new friends and family, as you journey through these chapters, take in the wisdom, absorb the lessons, and allow the transfiguration to unfold. Together, let's rekindle the essence of genuine human connection, rediscover the art of true love, and navigate the complex landscape of relationships with clarity, dignity, and purpose.

1
CONFESSIONS:
Breaking Free from the Chains of "Too Cool To LOVE"

In my many tumultuous cycles of self-discovery and personal growth, I found myself breaking free from the confines of Too Cool To LOVE. Metaphorically, I liken it to a daring escape from the notorious Alcatraz prison. I embarked on a journey of self-adjudication, propelled by a desperate need to live and find true freedom. The guards of misrepresentation, mistrust, and abuse no longer held me captive as I realized that loving oneself is the fundamental key to unlocking the beauty of life, and the essence of genuine love.

I was coiled in the darkness of deceit and dysfunction for far too long. Free from the grips of imprisonment, I jumped into the water and knew that I must find a way to survive the turbulent currents. Though my energy was low, I found solace in the strength of my renewed mind, and as I did so, the stench of death in the prison quickly gave way to fresh air, providing me with the opportunity to fill my lungs to capacity as I swam towards freedom. The 1.7-mile journey from Alcatraz to land seemed insurmountable, but my determination to reach solid ground remained unwavering.

As I delved deeper into the cold choppy waters, I grappled with the reasons behind my imprisonment within the confines of "Too Cool To LOVE." Doubts and uncertainties clouded my mind, causing me to question my identity. Along with that, I wanted to understand what led to this psychological incarceration? I confess, for years I identified as a pimp, a hustler, and a whore, and admit that I was all those things, everywhere, all at once. But at what point did I get so lost? And at what juncture did I become so despondent that I couldn't discern if I were a wiseman or a fool?

With each stroke towards freedom, I confronted the memories that ravaged my soul. I faced the pain I had caused others, the hearts I had broken, and the wreckage I left in my wake. The weight of my transgressions threatened to choke my stride, and with death looming, I began to imagine a world without my destructive influence.

Yet, it was through this process of reflection and redemption that I found the courage to envision a different future—one where I could use the lessons I was learning during my escape to help others break the chains of relationship bondage.

Too Cool To LOVE

I swam with every ounce of strength, my stride cutting through the water with determination. The waves crashed against me, testing my resolve, but I refused to falter. As I propelled myself through the tumultuous waters, I couldn't help but reflect on the journey that brought me here. Jumping into those treacherous currents was a symbolic act of liberation, a declaration that I was ready to confront my past and embrace a new path.

With each splash of water on my body, I felt the weight of my confessions being washed away. The act of acknowledging my transgressions and taking accountability cleansed my spirit, allowing me to leave behind the prison of destructive behaviors and toxic relationships.

Finally, the moment arrived when a powerful wave propelled me onto the shores of freedom. Solid ground beneath my feet, I stood tall and took a deep breath, relishing the taste of newfound independence. The experience transformed me, leaving me wiser and more resilient than ever before.

With the echoes of Alcatraz fading behind me, I embraced the notion that self-love and relationship salvation are interconnected. By acknowledging my past mistakes and actively working to break free from unhealthy patterns, I had embarked on a journey of personal growth and self-actualization. I stood there, basking in the warmth of the sun, knowing that I had the strength, courage, and heart to forge a different path.

Too Cool To LOVE

Now that I am here, I recognize that most people of today are experiencing some level of psychological, spiritual or social warfare. The world and its inhabitants have become disoriented, imprisoned behind the bars of entitlement and instant gratification. My hope is that this book offers you both a clear path forward and the tools to help you find your stride and regain your footing on solid ground.

Consider "Too Cool To LOVE" as your new place of refuge, a safe zone where you can invest time in self-reflection and exploration. By immersing yourself in its pages, you will uncover the depths of who you are and all that you can become. It will help you regain control over your life and make informed choices that align with your values and aspirations.

I implore you to embark on a journey of self-discovery, understanding the construct of your past to shed light on your present psychological makeup. This self-awareness is vital in facing and ultimately overcoming the challenge of acknowledging your past transgressions. By doing so, you empower yourself and pave the way for a future defined by strength, wisdom, and liberation.

Upon completing the lessons within this study guide, you will realize that there is no room and zero tolerance for destructive influences in your life. Through this process, you will find peace within yourself and create boundaries that safeguard your well-being.

Remember, my friend, that this book is merely a guide—a companion on your personal odyssey towards breaking free from the chains of "Too Cool To LOVE." The real power lies within you, in your willingness to confront your past, and embrace your truth.

As you immerse yourself in the stories, insights, and exercises provided in this book, I hope you discover the strength, courage, and wisdom to embark on your own transformative journey. May you find liberation, authenticity, and deep, meaningful connections that bring you joy and fulfillment.

With love and blessings, I wish you a profound life-changing experience as you embark on the path of self-love and freedom.

2

WHAT IS LOVE?:

Too Cool To Understand It

Before we delve into what "Too Cool to LOVE" means, let's first explore the concept of love and clarify its meaning. As we embark on this journey, let me set the tone for how I'd like you to experience this question and the entire book. Throughout this 15-chapter exploration, you will encounter references to music. As a musician, I firmly believe that sound has the ability to paint vivid pictures, amplify our thoughts, and intensify our emotions. The music and messages intertwined within this study guide create a space intended to ignite your psyche and conscience. So, from time to time, take my suggestion to pause, step away from reading, and let the curated playlist stimulate the therapy and transformation within you. This process will subtly unlock other realms of your heart, mind, and soul.

Allow me to introduce you to a song by a young man named J1 that I met some years ago. The song is titled "What Is Love?" To set the mood and evoke the right emotions for this

Too Cool To LOVE

lesson, I encourage you to open the "TooCoolToLove" playlist on Spotify and listen to "What Is Love?" by JHNJLN. This musical composition serves as a backdrop for this chapter, guiding us towards answering the question, "What is Love?"

Some of the lyrics of the song are below and resonate with our quest:

What is Love?

Help me describe it?

Where's the Love?

Has anybody seen it?

Who is Love?

Does anybody know it?

Got to find out where it is before I break…

These questions carry immense power. The artist expresses the need to understand and describe love. He wonders if others have witnessed or grasped its essence. The most poignant aspect of the lyrics suggest that a breaking point occurs because the artist has not found, seen or experienced love. Well how about you? Do you lack a harmonious balance of love in your life, or perhaps more curiously I ask, have you ever experienced or felt love at all?

Individuals who are "Too Cool To LOVE" typically carry scars from rough encounters with love or have been misguided about love's true nature from the start. The goal of this book is to mend the many wounds and scars of the past, and provide tools and resources to move you into a future that amplifies love and resilience. With many foundational questions and answers pending, let's start by overviewing a few popular quotes or descriptions about love that are prevalent in today's culture, then I will add layers of helpful information along the way.

- LOVE is GOD: I'm on board with this perspective.

- LOVE makes the world go round: Yes, I agree with this timeless notion.

- LOVE is when two people care for one another and would do anything to protect the other: That resonates as a genuine understanding of love.

- LOVE is helping those less fortunate: Absolutely! This compassionate aspect of love is truly admirable.

- LOVE is a serious mental disease: Don't be thrown off by this one. There is an element of truth in it.

In addition to these general descriptions about love, we could go as far reaching as examining the classical writings and statements of philosophers like Plato, Aristotle, and many others. If you were to consult AI, Google or Siri about the meaning of love, you would discover that love can be described and categorized in numerous ways.

But, as we progress towards finding the answer to what love is, it would help if we first look towards understanding the seven different types of love.

Ancient Greek studies suggest there are eight types of love, but their eighth speaks to obsession and jealousy, which we will leave out (for now) for the purposes of establishing a more warm and fuzzy feeling of love. Obsession plays a powerful role, and we will certainly address it later.

Here are the seven different types of love along with a brief explanation:

- **Eros:** This is often considered romantic or passionate love. It embodies intense desire, attraction, and physical longing. Eros is the type of love that ignites flames of passion and infatuation between individuals.

- **Philia:** This is the love of friendship and camaraderie. Philia represents deep affection, loyalty, and mutual respect shared among friends. It is characterized by a strong bond and a sense of shared experiences and trust.

- **Storge:** This type of love is the natural affection that exists within families, such as the love between parents and children or among siblings. Storge is a deep, unconditional love that arises from familiarity, comfort, and a sense of belonging.

- **Agape:** Agape is selfless, unconditional love. It transcends personal desires and expectations, focusing on the well-being and happiness of others. Agape love is often associated with acts of kindness, compassion, and altruism.

- **Ludus:** Ludus refers to playful, flirtatious love. It encompasses the lighthearted, joyful interactions between individuals. Ludus' love is characterized by teasing, laughter, and the excitement of early romantic pursuits.

- **Pragma:** Pragma is practical, enduring love. It is a deep understanding and commitment between partners built on shared values, compatibility, and long-term goals. Pragma love involves conscious effort and compromise to maintain a lasting relationship.

- **Philautia:** Philautia is self-love, but it can be understood in two distinct ways. One form of philautia is unhealthy self-centeredness and narcissism. However, the positive form of philautia is self-compassion, self-acceptance, and a healthy sense of self-worth. Cultivating self-love allows us to love others more authentically.

By understanding the nuances and dynamics of these different types of love, we can gain a deeper appreciation for the complexities of love itself and how it manifests in our lives. Despite the countless studies and tales of Greek gods and relationship poets, the true essence of love often remains veiled behind its own fortress, and to some extent, has become constrained or confined. But love is too immense and vibrant to be stifled by anything. And unadulterated love should never be excluded from your expectations of relationships or your pursuit of emotional fulfillment. In order to push love forward, we must redirect our focus and pursue a new strategic agenda to get your life and love to run together on the track.

When we contemplate love's significance, we realize that it permeates every aspect of human existence. Love serves as an intrinsic power source, driving the essence of all that is good. Peace, satisfaction, and happiness spring forth from love. Love is essential and the key to achieving balance and fulfillment in life.

With that in mind, let's begin to add on more layers of information and things for you to consider as we contemplate love's meaning and usefulness.

Too Cool To LOVE

Love as a Universal Force:

Love, at its core, is a universal force that penetrates every corner of our being. It is a boundless energy that connects us to one another, to the world around us, and to something greater than ourselves. Love is the underlying fabric that weaves together the intricate tapestry of human relationships, creating bonds that transcend time, distance, and circumstance.

Love as an Emotion:

Love is a complex and multifaceted emotion. It encompasses a range of feelings, from the euphoric highs of passion and infatuation to the tender warmth of deep affection and care. Love has the power to stir our souls, ignite our hearts, and bring immense joy and fulfillment to our lives. It is a profound emotional experience that can elicit vulnerability, strength, and a deep sense of connection with another person.

Love as a Choice:

While love often begins as a feeling, it evolves into a conscious choice we make every day. Love is not merely a fleeting emotion; it is a commitment to care, support, and nurture the wellbeing of another person. It is a deliberate decision to prioritize the needs and happiness of someone else, even when it requires sacrifice or compromise. Love is an ongoing journey of choosing to be there for someone, to stand by their side through both the joys and the hardships.

Too Cool To LOVE

Love as a Transformative Power:

Love possesses a profound transformative power. It has the ability to heal wounds, mend broken hearts, and inspire personal growth. Love can dissolve barriers and prejudices while bridging divides. It is through love that we discover our true selves and unlock the depths of our compassion and empathy. Love has the potential to shape us into better versions of ourselves, fostering kindness, understanding, and acceptance.

Love as Connection and Unity:

At its essence, love is about connection and unity. It is the invisible thread that links us all, reminding us of our shared humanity. Love transcends differences and reminds us that we are all interconnected beings, each deserving of compassion, respect, and love. It is through love that we forge deep bonds of friendship, nurture familial relationships, and cultivate a sense of belonging within communities.

Love as Growth and Expansion:

Love is not static; it is dynamic and ever-evolving. It encourages personal growth, inviting us to step outside our comfort zones, challenge our beliefs, and embrace new experiences. Love propels us to expand our capacity for empathy, understanding, and forgiveness. It pushes us to become better versions of ourselves and inspires us to strive for greater heights in our relationships, careers, and personal aspirations.

While I believe that love is a mix of all of the aforementioned. I feel strongly that love's biggest and most important ingredient is *TRUTH*.

Love is Truth:

When we contemplate love, it becomes evident that truth plays an integral role. Love, in its expression and reception, necessitates confidence and a sense of safety, which can only be achieved through trust. Love is synonymous with trust, and trust requires truth.

Truth becomes a relationship's greatest ally, while its absence becomes its worst enemy. Without truth and honesty, love cannot thrive. Love supported with truth fosters emotional stability and brings about profound peace. First, you must be truthful and honest with yourself, accepting the truth about who you are and what truly fulfills you. It is equally crucial to extend that truthfulness to others. Additionally, learning to accept the truth about the people in your life is vital. Also, expressing the truth, even when it disappoints or unsettles others, is imperative for maintaining peace and balance in your circle of life. The foundation of truth and your unwavering commitment to it is where you must begin and take a stand.

Truth carries tremendous responsibility. If you claim to love someone but lack clarity and fail to disclose your true intentions, it will likely lead to disastrous consequences. Lies and cover-ups that disregard another person's well-being can cause irreparable harm, comparable to pushing them off a cliff. It begs the question: Will this person survive the fall? Will they be left with shattered dignity and deep psychological scars? Or will it be a fate worse than death as love betrayals have the power to extinguish one's belief in love itself?

For these reasons and more, it is absolutely necessary to establish a value system centered around Responsible and Responsive Truth.

Responsible Truth ~ entails taking ownership and responsibility, acknowledging that trust and truth underpin every aspect of your life.

Responsive Truth ~ requires taking a leadership role that commits you to respond to the needs of others, even when they differ from your own agenda.

The purpose of responsible and responsive truth is to guide you, and use them as your barometer for every relationship consideration. Do not let your truth, or lack thereof, become the push or the bullet that destroys someone's self-worth and self-esteem. Always operate in truth with the intention of uplifting and building positive relationships with those you come in contact with, rather than exacerbate or destroy them.

Once you embrace responsible and responsive truth, your life with love can begin to take on its true shape. Making a firm commitment to align with, and initiate the principles established in the chapter thus far, marks a significant first step.

So the truth is, love is complex. There are a myriad of feelings, emotions and circumstances to manage related to creating a solid base of love in your life. Yet, the one thing that is consistent across all paths that lead to love, is truth. By living your truth you no longer have to conform to someone else's desires; instead, you create and shape your own path. The gratification that comes from living at this level of truth and self-ownership is immeasurable.

Ultimately, my goal is to empower men and women worldwide to experience true love and transcend the games, lies and emotional starvation prevalent in today's relationship culture. My aim is to center and equip individuals by giving them the tools to discern and manage various types of relationships—be it a relationship with yourself (Philia), romantic love (Eros), or love among friends (Philautia), and others, I am fully committed to helping you, break free from the constraints of being "Too Cool To LOVE."

We all have work to do. It's time to don our armor as warriors of love to uplift and defend love's freedom. When love is unencumbered, it fills your heart, soul, mind, and body with a vibrant palette of emotions. Love's synergy should resonate in your life like the morning sun surging across the blue sky, racing towards kissing a restful moon at night. While this description may sound somewhat like a movie script, love has the remarkable power to unlock boundless possibilities and create real life stories that offer you a wondrous tapestry of opportunities.

Too Cool To LOVE

By the time you complete all the chapters within this Too Cool To LOVE study guide, you will very likely emerge motivated, liberated, joyful, and free. This will only happen if you commit to digging in and do the work, for love is not passive. Remember, if any of your current relationships lack unmitigated, responsible and responsive truth, I strongly suggest that you leave such relationships as soon as possible. Trust me, it will never flourish or mature as it should, and you cannot afford to waste any more of your precious time.

Once you grasp the power and unity that truth provides, you will find that absolute clarity is walking with you on your journey towards true love.

3
Truth:
Too Cool to Acknowledge It

Please carefully buckle in, we are about to embark on a journey that may stir up some heart wrenching discomfort within you. It is a journey that invites you to examine the role of truth in your life and relationships. When I speak about relationships, it is not limited to romantic partnerships alone. Truth must be the core principle that underpins every aspect of your existence. And you must no longer allow anyone who possesses a penchant for lies and deceit to remain in your life or within your inner circles. Such individuals disrupt and inflict pain upon you and you may find yourself living a life veiled in deception.

Beneath the surface of lies, games, secrets, and manipulations is the wreckage of your daily existence. Though you may wear a smile, make excuses, and overlook the obvious, internally you are fractured, and the Van Gogh painting of your life is about to fall down from the wall and shatter into pieces. The truth is, the weight of all the deception and relationship falsehoods have brought you to your breaking point.. If you are like most people, you have mastered the art of disguise (a Too Cool To LOVE trait) and things appear picture perfect to those looking from the outside in.. You likely feel you should be nominated for an Oscar based on your exceptional performances in portraying the happy person, the good friend, or the loving partner. It is astonishing how you manage to endure this charade day after day. However, this cannot continue. It is time to cease allowing people to deceive you, cover up the truth (yours and theirs), and construct false narratives to either take advantage of you or keep you in the dark for their own unscrupulous purposes. It is time to awaken from the darkness and refuse to be a punching bag for manipulation.

Let's look at this from a visual perspective. Take a moment and imagine your body in a boxing ring, enduring relentless blows from a heavyweight champion like Mike Tyson, one body blow after another. Close your eyes and truly see and feel the impact. Your body would be left broken, ravaged, perhaps incapacitated or even lifeless. In this analogy, the lies, deceit and manipulation are the puncher, and the strikes may be coming from your spouse, friends, lover, or family members, or maybe, it's even you. Regardless of where they are coming from, the continued onslaught of lies and trickery will break you down and extinguish your life. Person to person and/or internal battering is neither healthy nor sustainable and by permitting such abusive behavior, you are likely living with profound depression, the effects of which we all know too well.

Accepting a life of lies and residing under the influence of manipulation sets the stage for immense disappointment and failure. Whether consciously or unconsciously, the evidence shows you are living a life where you are undervalued. This must not be allowed to persist. Stop allowing people to take shots at you by controlling your life through lies and deceit, or simply being irresponsible with matters of the heart. Embracing lies or accepting a relationship founded upon falsehoods and unfulfilled promises is the deepest, darkest, and most egregious way of disrespecting yourself.

Perhaps the core of this lack of respect, and thus the source of your pain, lies in your attempts to rationalize and live a life alongside those who are not true to you, because they are not committed to giving you what you actually want and need. It could also be a situation where you are presenting a façade to others, a lifestyle that is not genuine or authentic. Regardless of the direction, these types of deception cause your relationships to hemorrhage and ultimately they bleed out. Happiness becomes ephemeral, and love cannot endure.

Therefore, you must be clear with the people around you. Push them to understand your values and convictions. Ensure that they accept and respect your truth. And if they cannot accept it, that is okay. When you establish clear boundaries, they will be compelled to respect them. There is immeasurable power and freedom in embracing truth, especially your own.

With that said, let's explore the fundamental reasons and the invaluable benefits truth brings to your life. Once we grasp these 7 foundational principles, we can delve into how truth influences the relationships between men and women in today's social climate.

The 7 Laws of Truth:

1. Truth lacks ignorance

In the realm of truth, ignorance has no place. When truth is present, there is no absence of knowledge or information. It provides the necessary data to make important decisions and take appropriate action. Just like knowing that 25 pennies equals a quarter and 4 quarters make a dollar–having access to truth empowers you to clearly navigate life's complexities. In relationships, lacking the basic foundation of truth leaves you in a state of ignorance, making it difficult to make informed decisions and find clarity. Truth eliminates ignorance and offers transparency, allowing you to move forward with confidence and security.

2. Truth will guide you by establishing your steps

Information, whether it is based on truth or lies, is like a trail of breadcrumbs. The critical question is, where does this trail lead? Birds instinctively follow breadcrumbs without considering the destination. But if the bird knew that the end of the trail meant certain death, would it still continue? Similarly, following breadcrumbs of lies and deceit makes you comparable to a clueless bird, ultimately leading to your demise. Instead, ensure that you follow a trail of truth. When truth serves as your guide you will be led toward more positive outcomes. While truth may sometimes be painful and necessitate difficult decisions or changes in direction, it provides a more peaceful and stable journey. Insisting on truth builds a solid foundation for your relationships, serving as a reliable roadmap for the paths ahead.

3. Truth is your advocate for peace

Truth assumes the role of a soldier, steadfastly guarding your inner peace. It stands as a vigilant warrior, protecting you from nefarious forces. With truth by your side, your fortress remains impenetrable. Lies and deceit are kept at bay, ensuring your peace of mind remains undisturbed. Truth advocates for your well-being and shields you from harm, providing the sanctuary you need to thrive.

4. Truth will confirm

Truth acts as the ultimate tool for confirming facts and dispelling doubts, enabling you to make informed decisions. You can measure and confirm truth against two critical elements: God's word and a person's actions. When these align, you are likely to experience a deep sense of affirmation within your spirit. Incorporating faith and aligning with the word of God, provides a solid foundation for making fruitful decisions. Your spiritual reference point serves as a barometer for truth, confirming its presence and guiding your path. Authenticating truth through action and alignment with your spiritual beliefs strengthens your conviction and leads to greater clarity.

5.   Truth pre-determines your future

When you align yourself with truth and surround yourself with individuals who embrace it, you become an active participant in shaping your destiny. Living and operating in truth sets the stage for a bright and exuberant future. Your experiences, the quality of your relationships, and the peace of mind you cultivate are predetermined by the positive or negative choices you make. This spiritual law of reaping what you sow highlights the importance of planting seeds of truth, nurturing them with the confidence that truth sustains positive growth. By aligning with truth, you can cultivate a life characterized by peace, free from the pressures of relationship falsehoods and unnecessary depression.

6.   Truth will embolden

To be emboldened means to feel empowered and confident in making choices. With truth as your foundation, you possess the strength and wisdom to navigate life's challenges and make the right choices. Having access to all the facts through truth instills a sense of safety and trust in your abilities. Embracing truth gives you the authority to assert yourself, just like a police officer who has the right to ask, enforce, and assert boundaries. The power of truth allows you to be bold, inspiring, motivating, and exciting.

7.   Truth builds emotional closeness and intimacy

Prepare to be astonished by the intimacy and closeness that truth fosters. When truth becomes the binding force in your relationship, confidence and trust soar. This newfound level of trust enhances not only the emotional connection but also the level of intimacy and passion between partners. It can be a remarkable life story when two spirits, souls, and bodies truly unite through honesty. This level of comfort and connection unlocks a passion that surpasses expectations.

Break time: Here is where you can take my suggestion to pause and recalibrate your thoughts, feelings and emotions with music. If allowed, it may positively infuse you and help as you continue the transformative process.

Go to the TooCoolToLove playlist on Spotify and listen to "Honesty" by Pink Sweat$. The song beautifully captures the closeness and intimacy that all relationships seek, desire and deserve. Building on truth establishes the type of bonding that enables you to let go of inhibitions and trust your soul, mind, and body within the relationship. Mutual trust is the key that unlocks profound peace and unmeasurable experiences. Truth and honesty serves as the teacher, helping you construct a solid framework for affection and fostering deep emotional connections.

Unveiling the Reality:

It is essential for me to emphasize that this book was initially intended as a self-help guide for men, aiming to address toxic masculinity and the need for men to confront deceptive, corrosive, malapropos behaviors and the mindset of being so-called players, pimps and hustlers.

However, it has become evident that both men and women need to be part of the conversation and solutions. And we all should accept and embrace the fact that the current dating landscape is mutually at a "State of Emergency". Nonetheless, this does not change the facts nor the reality that trust and faith in men continue to erode.

I think we all understand by now that the traditional theme of the 1950s does not apply. Women no longer portray docile and trusting housewives. Women have gained leverage and empowerment, which is a remarkable development. It is also essential to acknowledge that many women have had to evolve and develop dominant egos to protect themselves and provide for their own needs. This shift in dynamics has dramatically changed the playing field.

It would also be prudent for men to recognize that women have the capacity to play a heavier and colder hand when it comes to games, deception and abuse, and the truth is, most men are ill-prepared to navigate this new reality. But at this juncture, it is crucial to understand that both men and women need to embrace the value of truth, respect and loyalty so that we can all avoid falling into the trap of being "Too Cool To LOVE."

As we continue this journey, I must caution and inform you that the questions and the unraveling process ahead may be challenging to confront. There are some profound truths that need to be acknowledged and addressed. And if you are ready, let's dive deeper into the questions that will help you uncover your truth and the truth in your relationships.

What is your Truth?

The questions below are meant to provoke self-reflection and explore the impact of truth in your life and any external relationships. Take a moment to truly absorb these questions and consider how they make you feel. If the questions or answers don't bother or affect you personally, then perhaps consider how other parties involved would feel or be affected if everyone knew the truth, the whole truth and nothing but the truth.

10 questions to help see things clearly:

- 1. Are you content with being just an occasional sex partner?

- 2. Does the person you are involved with know about your marital status or other heart-string commitments?

- 3. Does your partner know you were a victim of abuse, and how it affects you today?

- 4. Does your partner know about your financial instability?

- 5. Have you told someone you love them when you know deep down that you don't?

- 6. Are you dissatisfied with the sex life with your partner, and perhaps afraid to express issues of dissatisfaction with them?

- 7. Are you currently married but deep down you want a divorce?

- 8. Are you engaging in drug use or perhaps dealing with an addiction without your partner's knowledge?

- 9. Does your partner or friends know your sexual preferences or orientation?

- 10. Are you certain about the paternity of a child?

These specific questions may or may not directly apply to your situation, but they serve as examples to guide you towards clarity and truth in your relationships and can be used as your measuring stick. I encourage you to create your own Top 10 list of questions that resonate with your life and relationship profiles. By identifying and addressing these questions, you can pave the way for the balance and clarity you deserve, and set the stage for the life you truly desire.

My Top 10 (create your personalized questions):

1._____
2._____
3._____
4._____
5._____
6._____
7._____
8._____
9._____
10._____

Once you have asked yourself the tough questions and discover your truth, it will be time to evaluate those in your outer circle. At some point it should become routine for you to hold everyone accountable for truth and clear communication. If people want to be a part of your life, both they and you must commit to a relationship that fosters respect, peace, and resolutions through truth. Nothing can be more critical for the baseline of your relationships.

Let's be clear: this journey requires tremendous effort. However, the payoff is immeasurable. Embracing unmitigated truth will provide genuine opportunities for you to experience true love, both with yourself and others. Truth is the foundation upon which all relationships should be built, and it is the path to a fulfilling and authentic life. Without truth, integrity and unselfish love, the Eros partnership you may crave will remain elusive.

Food for Thought: The Consequences of Deception

After exploring the depths of this chapter about truth, it is necessary to reflect on the profound consequences of consciously lying, deceiving and manipulating others. If you choose to persist in such destructive behaviors, or worse, accept them, not only are you endangering the lives of those around you, you are also compromising your own virtue. In this case your relationship/s meet the nature of the insidious "Spinochordodes Tellini". The only question is, which role do you play?

The Spinochordodes Tellini is a parasitic worm that infiltrates its host, feeding off it until it reaches maturity. Once fully grown, it manipulates the host's behavior, compelling it to leap to its death. Similarly, individuals who thrive on lies and deceit are capable of inflicting irreparable harm, causing their victims to suffer greatly. They will stop at nothing to advance their own selfish interests, even if it means destroying the lives and well-being of others.

This grim reality serves as a stark reminder of the dire consequences associated with deception. It is a plea for you to reconsider your actions and the impact they have on both yourself and those you interact with. The power to inflict harm through dishonesty is a burden that should never be taken lightly. So, I implore you to examine your own motives and the potential harm you may be causing. Embrace truth, for it is the key to preserving your self-esteem, upholding your moral compass, and fostering genuine connections with others. Only by rejecting deceit and embracing honesty can we hope to build a world based on trust, respect, and true love.

Remember, truth will always prevail, and the consequences of deception are far too great to bear. Your actions have the power to transform not only yourself but also the world around you. So choose the path of honor and integrity and become an advocate for truth in all aspects of your life.

4
Too Cool To LOVE:
Too Bruised to Love

So far we have explored various topics to gain a deeper understanding of what love truly means. Now that you are armed with the knowledge and value placed on a life filled with love, truth and respect, we can now begin to explore the concept of being "Too Cool To LOVE".

So, who or what exactly is "Too Cool To LOVE"?

Definition: "Too Cool To LOVE" refers to an individual that has the ability to conceal the inadequacies or deceptive behaviors that hinder or discourage them from establishing love in a committed relationship. This physiological disposition allows a person to mask their true identity and avoid experiencing emotions and, as a result, prevents or blocks them from experiencing genuine love.

"Too Cool" characteristics can manifest as either a conscious or subconscious personality trait, or it can even stem from deep-rooted psychological issues. Regardless of the underlying cause, this behavior can wreak havoc on those looking to establish healthy and balanced relationships.

Being "Too Cool" has little to do with being cool in the traditional sense. In this context, "Cool" speaks to playing it cool, the cover-up with a smile. Someone who typically hides behind the mask of a mis-aligned agenda or ill intentions against trust and emotional stability.

But no need to worry, this study guide is here to help you identify and overcome the masks, because your very life may depend on it. You will be given the tools to stay sharp, alert, vigilant and keenly aware of the type of people who inflict pain delivered by a beautiful, yet venomous smile.

To initiate corrective action, you must first confront some challenging questions. Like, what are the aspects of yourself that you are concealing? And, what are the unresolved issues or personality traits that hinder you or your partner from establishing a meaningful relationship based on truth?

Committing to truth and fostering positive moral values is merely the first step. The real challenge lies in delving into the psychological traits that contribute to such detrimental "Too Cool To LOVE" behaviors.

Furthermore, what drives people to cover up, fake it, and be dishonest with themselves and others? In many ways, being "Too Cool" represents a psychological dysfunction that may necessitate the guidance of a spiritual leader or life coach to overcome it. However, I hope that the insights and lessons provided in this book will prove to be a sufficient starting place, equipping you with the necessary resources to break free from these patterns, and/or helping you to recognize them so you can quickly escape when presented.

It is of great importance that you elevate your consciousness and make transformative changes that will enhance your personal and dating life.

The ultimate purpose of this book, this study guide, is to awaken the minds and hearts of men and women globally, propelling them towards a life characterized by truth, clarity, wholeness, and overall excellence, and this work starts at the individual level, with you.

To embark on this transformative journey, it is crucial to understand the history and origins of being "Too Cool." Many individuals who exhibit "Too Cool To LOVE" behaviors have experienced varying degrees of heartbreak and disappointment during their formative years (typically between the ages of 9 and 17). These formative years, or what I like to call the "MOLDING" years, hold tremendous significance. They serve as the training playground, where emotions start to intertwine with meaningful experiences. Factors such as divorce and single parenting often play a pivotal role during this phase.

It comes as no surprise that teenagers grapple with various levels of depression, and sadly, suicide becomes a part of this narrative. I know because I was one of them. However, some of us were fortunate enough to navigate through the challenges, finding a delicate balance and preserving our sanity as we transitioned into adulthood.

For many young adults (perhaps you), the process of forming personality traits and inappropriate behaviors occurred amidst experiences of infidelity, incest, rape, physical or verbal abuse, most often within the confines of our own homes.

Others who exhibit "Too Cool" tendencies developed these habits as adults, stemming from a series of unfulfilling or hurtful relationships. In many cases, heartbreak resulting from disappointing relationships can be a valuable learning experience, particularly during youth. It allows one to quickly identify what to avoid and establish as boundaries and standards for the future. However, as we grow older, the process becomes more challenging. We encounter increasingly distressing experiences, absorbing pre-existing off-key behavioral traits. Our survival instincts compel us to construct superficial walls and hide behind the facade of a self-induced persona or public perception.

Subconsciously, beneath these layers, we seek ways to guard and protect ourselves. Escaping reality or evading hurt and pain becomes second nature, leading individuals to cover things up and adopt a "Too Cool" demeanor.

None of us entered this world as "Too Cool To LOVE." We did not come into existence with a predisposition to camouflage our emotions or inadequacies, nor with a callousness or

Too Cool To LOVE

anger that drives us to avoid or even destroy relationships. Being "Too Cool" is a learned behavior stemming from painful experiences during our formative years or adult relationships, or perhaps a combination of both.

Whether you are a curious teenager exploring your sense of self or a seasoned adult seeking personal growth, it is mandatory that you conduct an honest assessment of your life history to date. Let's examine some of your negative traits and behaviors, and begin the process of identifying their origins. Once you gain a deeper understanding and learn to confront them, you can gradually eliminate the "Too Cool To LOVE" elements from your personal life and / or your external relationships.

Below is a general checklist designed to help you identify the Too Cool To LOVE characteristics and learned behaviors that may be part of your makeup or history. It is important to approach this exercise with deep thought and honesty, allowing yourself to uncover any hidden aspects that may be holding you back from experiencing true love.

Take your time here. Writing down notes about yourself and your relationships can be a truly eye-opening experience.

Too Insecure:

Have you been subjected to negative comments from parents, loved ones, or friends, causing you to doubt your abilities or attractiveness? This common experience can lead to self-doubt and lack of support during your formative years. Additionally, if you have experienced abuse during past relationships, it may have further contributed to your insecurities.

Insecurity manifests in various forms and hues, making it one of the most formidable challenges to conquer. Regrettably, it is also glaringly apparent to others, putting you at a higher risk of enduring further mistreatment. Those with predatory strength possess an innate ability to detect and exploit fear and vulnerability, making you susceptible to becoming their prey. Insecurities significantly hinder the establishment of meaningful relationships. Exercise utmost caution when dealing with this issue and don't hesitate to seek professional assistance if necessary. Overcoming insecurity can be challenging, but also a life changing experience towards establishing healthy relationships, and it can be done.

Check here as applicable:

Questions	Yes	No
I am currently a little insecure and I recognize I need some support.		
I struggled with this and believe I have overcome it.		

I have struggled with this, but am aware of it and working through it.		
This does not apply to me.		

If elements of insecurity apply to me, how has or is this affecting my relationships?
1.
2.
3.

Besides myself, who is or perhaps who was hurt by this behavior?
1.
2.
3.

Too Bougie:

Do you have a tendency to prioritize materialistic pursuits and associate love with wealth and status? Are you solely focused on finding a partner with financial means, overlooking potential connections based on genuine compatibility?

First and foremost, it's perfectly fine to appreciate and enjoy first-class service and a luxurious lifestyle. I certainly do. However, it can be beneficial to maintain a balance between your pursuit of wealth and comfort and other important aspects of life.

Too Cool To LOVE

It can also be consequential not to realize that there are many talented and accomplished individuals who will find success independently, without relying on you. Meanwhile, those who have substantial financial wealth are often preoccupied with their own pursuits or simply uninterested in forming a connection with you. Apart from fleeting moments of passion and the occasional display of your captivating charisma, you offer little substance.

Keep in mind that individuals with true power and fortune seldom commit themselves to mediocrity. If you aspire to enter into a relationship that is akin to finding a pot of gold, you should possess some "gold" of your own, or the potential to acquire it. Even if you have achieved personal success, exercise caution when engaging in superficial conversations and showcasing material possessions that merely serve to create a facade.

Believe me when I say that you'll experience many more triumphs, and create valuable opportunities if you open your heart and focus on the essential elements of a genuine connection.

Check here as applicable:

Question	Yes	No
I am currently a bit bougie.		

I have struggled with this, but am aware of it and working through it.		
I struggled with this and believe I have overcome it.		
This does not apply to me.		

If being over-the-top bougie applies to me, how has or is this affecting my relationships?
1.
2.
3.

Besides myself, who is or perhaps who was hurt by this behavior?
1.
2.
3.

Too much history (baggage/damage):
Are past experiences causing you to make biased judgments about potential partners or preventing you from fully trusting in new relationships? If you have experienced abuse or traumatic events, it is important to address and heal from these wounds before entering into new relationships.

That said, it is wise to be prudent when it comes to meeting new people. However, if you enter into new relationships without addressing or letting go of your emotional baggage, it will become incredibly challenging to trust anyone fully. It's key to acknowledge your past and confront it, or at the very least, gain a deep understanding of how it affects you before embarking on a new relationship.

If you find yourself in the aforementioned category and decide to take a chance on building a relationship, I recommend delicately opening up about your past issues and current baggage with your partner. They are not obligated to stay, but by sharing your truth and providing them with an honest understanding of your history, you set the foundation for a more authentic connection. Should the relationship progress, working together to navigate and heal from past traumas can bring about significant growth and positive change.

Let's be clear: the idea of carrying emotional baggage is not appealing to anyone, and it's vital you make an effort to resolve as much of it as possible beforehand. Attempting to conceal your baggage is not a viable solution. In either case, facing and addressing it head-on from the beginning will save you valuable time and energy. Learn to confront and release the burdens of your history, and you will find yourself in a much healthier and fulfilling place.

Check here as applicable:

Question	Yes	No

I had a bad/complicated history and I recognize I need some support.		
I have struggled with this, but am aware of it and working through it.		
I struggled with this and believe I have overcome it.		
This does not apply to me.		

If elements of an unhealthy history apply to me, how has or is this affecting my relationships?
1.
2.
3.

Besides myself, who is or perhaps who was hurt by this behavior?
1.
2.
3.

Too much power:
Do you exploit your position of power or influence to take advantage of others, whether sexually or otherwise? While having power and influence is not inherently negative, it is important to recognize the responsibility that comes with it. The

misuse of power can lead to manipulation and emotional harm in relationships.

Clearly, wealth itself is not a bad thing. However, it is important to recognize that there can be many falsehoods lurking beneath the surface of power. It's a well-known fact that those who acquire great wealth often wield significant influence and can dictate the rules of the game. Unfortunately, these rules often allow them to deceive others and derive satisfaction from their deceit. They feel entitled to lie and devalue others, leaving little room for scrutiny or questioning.

The allure of the power-lifestyle is undeniable, and it holds a certain awe-inspiring quality. But don't be deceived. Even the most powerful individuals crave deep emotional connections and yearn for true love. The challenge lies in their struggle to navigate the complexities of control and manipulation that come with their influential positions.

This "Too Cool Power Life" often clouds their ability to recognize or appreciate genuine love, even when it is right in front of them. Control is a close companion of power and it can be the root cause of catastrophic emotional disasters. Its impact is not limited to the individuals at the receiving end—it can boomerang back to the very source of power.

Therefore, it is critical to exercise caution when you have influence and authority. Be mindful of how you use your power, understanding the potential consequences of throwing your weight around recklessly. Strive for balance and integrity, understanding that true love requires genuine emotional connections, unaffected by power dynamics.

Check here as applicable:

Question	Yes	No
I am a power mis-abuser. I recognize I need some support.		
I have struggled with this, but am aware of it and working through it.		
I struggled with this and believe I have overcome it.		
This does not apply to me.		

If elements of abuse of power apply to me, how has or is this affecting my relationships?

1.
2.
3.

Besides myself, who is or perhaps who was hurt by this behavior?

1.
2.
3.

Too pre-dispositioned:

Here are some examples of a pre-dispositioned mindset (list). What are yours?

Her list (must be):	*His list (must be):*
6'2" or taller	*College level-education*
Wealthy	*Latina or mixed*
No kids	*Have a good job*
6 Pack	*Gotta have a big booty*

Having a list of wants and desires is good and, in many ways, recommended. We all have an ideology of things we want, and that is perfectly healthy. There is nothing wrong with shooting for the stars and aspiring to what you desire.

However, it's important to recognize that finding the perfect match who checks off every item on your list is like winning the lottery. In reality, there are usually plenty of good relationship partners in your general environment to work with or choose from. By stepping away from a super rigid list, you open yourself up to genuine opportunities that may surprise you.

I'm not suggesting that you should completely discard your list. Instead, consider it as a flexible guide or outline that you can update from time to time based on new life experiences and opportunities. Allow yourself to be open to things that have potential, even if they don't perfectly align with every item on your list.

It's worth mentioning that at some point, you may have been attracted to certain individuals who didn't meet all the criteria on your list. Perhaps, you even cut off any emotions or potential for growth simply because they didn't fit your predefined expectations. By being more open-minded, you increase your chances of discovering fulfilling connections and experiences.

Remember, people who are unwilling to adapt and remain rigid in their pre-dispositioned mindset often find themselves older and alone, settling for far less than they ever would have considered years prior. Embrace the opportunity for growth and allow yourself to explore beyond the confines of a limited checklist.

Check here as applicable:

Question	Yes	No
I have a rigid pre-disposition and I recognize I need to loosen up.		
I have struggled with this, but am aware of it and working through it.		
I struggled with this and believe I have overcome it.		
This does not apply to me.		

If elements of pre-disposition apply to me, how has or how is this affecting my opportunity with relationships?
1.
2.
3.

Besides myself, who is or perhaps who was hurt by this behavior?
1.
2.
3.

Too much of a player:

Do you find yourself involved with multiple partners who believe they are the only one you're seeing? Do they hold the belief that the relationship has more significance to you than it actually does? With your skilled deception, do they lack a clear understanding and believe they are your sole focus? Are you like a superhero who can conceal calls, text messages, social media posts, and any evidence of other lovers in your life?

Perhaps you're so adept that you even maintain an entire secret family. My goodness.

I understand that in urban culture, the label "player" is sometimes used as a term of endearment. I get it. However, in a traditional sense, players have exhausted their playtime. There's no need for such behavior. The streetwise part of me recognizes that players are simply cowards, and therefore, I distance myself from them.

The essence behind being a player is unsightly. Intentional lies and deception in a relationship are among the cruelest ways to harm everyone involved, mostly yourself, and the lasting impact is indelible.

In your pursuit of love and obedience, I strongly advise you to be authentic with yourself and anyone you engage with, particularly in intimate relationships.

Yet, respectfully, if you're young or old and still enjoy exploring various connections, that can be a terrific phase of life - there's nothing inherently wrong with it. However, in that case, you need to be upfront and honest about it, leaving no room for ambiguity.

And here's a little secret for you. You might be surprised by how many positive responses you receive from your love interest when you're upfront and provide them with full disclosure. Honesty from the start goes a long way.

Break time: Here is where you can take my suggestion to pause and recalibrate your thoughts, feelings and emotions with music. If allowed, it may positively infuse you and help as you continue the transformative process.

Too Cool To LOVE

Head over to the TooCoolToLove playlist on Spotify and groove to the track "Grey Area" by Kaytranada. It will add a bounce and a little pick me before you continue.

Check here as applicable:

Question	Yes	No
I am still on the players' court playing.		
I have struggled with this, but am aware of it and working through it.		
I struggled with this and believe I have overcome it.		
This does not apply to me.		

If elements of being a player and heartbreak apply to me, how has or is this affecting my relationships?

1.
2.
3.

Besides myself, who is or perhaps who was hurt by this behavior?

1.
2.
3.

Too Cool To LOVE

Too much career:

Do you prioritize your career and workplace advancement above your relationship? Have you used your job as an excuse to stay busy and avoid starting a relationship or confronting the realities of your current one? Do you frequently find yourself uttering the phrase, "I'm busy"?

In pursuit of your ambitious business goals, have you allowed your relationship to suffer in the pursuit of power or fame? It's possible that you initially had a more balanced approach with your partner, but as your professional aspi-rations grew, you became out of sync. Have you veered away from your designated role of providing connection and joy in the relationship? Remember when you used to go to the movies, hold hands, travel, and enjoy innovative intimate moments, but now both of you are preoccupied and distant?

The truth is, as human beings, we rarely want to feel like there is something or someone else more important than us. Whether you're a billionaire with a packed schedule or a 9 to 5 employee, it's essential to make time to connect with your partner in order to cultivate the beautiful rewards of a fulfilling relationship. Regardless of whether you've achieved your career goals or are still on the path to their attainment, it's important to remain open to receiving and giving love. Being too consumed by busyness is a slow and inevitable destroyer of Eros love. Money and power have a way of leaving an empty void when there is no genuine connection or shared life experiences. You might achieve financial success, but what about love?

Too Cool To LOVE

Check here as applicable:

Question	Yes	No
I recognize I am not available, and balance is needed.		
I have struggled with this, but am aware of it and working through it.		
I struggled with this and believe I have overcome it.		
This does not apply to me.		

If elements of busyness apply to me, how has or how is this affecting my opportunity with relationships?
1.
2.
3.

Besides myself, who is or perhaps who was hurt by this behavior?
1.
2.
3.

These examples represent just a fraction of the venomous traits and behaviors associated with the various Too Cool To LOVE personality types. Any encounter with them can have a detrimental effect on your spirit and hinder the healthy development of your emotions.

It is climacteric to identify and acknowledge any inadequacies or deceptive behaviors within yourself and those around you as soon as possible. And while the pre-determined checklist provided was an example, it is necessary that you create a new list. With the knowledge you now have, your list should identify positive behaviors and characteristics that are germane to your well being and the overall probability for long term success with a relationship partner.

When compiling your lists, take into account that most of us possess some form of the "Too Cool", or "Too Something" character traits described herein. The key lies in acknowledging them, holding yourself accountable, and actively working to dismantle them on your own, and / or with your new love interest. This can help you create a more stable foundation and a better mental disposition for everyone involved, which saves valuable time.

In conclusion: the Too Cool To LOVE epidemic continues to spread rapidly, and it is further ignited by the pervasive influence of a 24/7 social media lifestyle. In today's digital age, it's easy to present a curated version of oneself to hide behind the countless options of internet apps and filters. As you may have already discovered, the people you meet online may not always be who or what they claim to be, so be aware of the mask-wearing marauders lurking behind the façades of Instagram, Tik Tok, or Match.com. As part of the remedy, go outside and do something that seems to be a thing of the past, meet people one on one, talk and be social.

Throughout this lesson, we have looked deep into the shadows, engaging in introspective soul-searching to uncover buried treasures within ourselves. Now you hold a set of new keys to your own transformation, and it should be compulsory to protect and lock down the precious jewels you have unearthed. Whether you purchased this book yourself or received it as a gift, there is a reason it has come into your hands. Its content aims to guide you in working through past ideologies, character flaws and paradigm shifts that prepare you to get to the other side.

Thank you for taking the necessary steps to rectify your behaviors, and honing your ability to discern and eliminate discriminatory actions and thoughts. And with that, the amount of pain you accept or inflict upon yourself and others will significantly diminish.

Moving forward, I am excited to believe that you feel a newfound strength, resilience, and acquired enough wisdom to help you navigate above the treacherous pitfalls inherent in the Too Cool To LOVE matrix.

Your future looks brighter, and life will be a more fulfilling journey because you are equipped with the tools needed to overcome any challenges that lie ahead.

5
The Toolbox:
Too Cool To Fix It

My Personal Story:

You do not need a crane to move a sheet of paper, nor would you use a hammer to catch a small fish. Effective completion of any task requires the proper tools. Working hard with the wrong tools will only exacerbate the situation, and will not solve your problems. Stop wasting valuable time and energy and work smarter not harder.

The purpose of this chapter is to encourage you to reflect on your history in order to help you better understand what tools were used to construct your belief systems, behavioral traits, and psychological disposition. You'll likely discover a direct correlation between the tools you've utilized in the past and the way you currently build your life and relationships.

Understanding the contents of your toolbox and the importance of periodically cleaning and recalibrating your tools is imperative. The relationship marketplace, expectations and requirements continuously change, necessitating the need for you to update and diversify your toolbox. If you plan to be relevant, and considered for relationship advancement on any level, this is pertinent.

Similar to how a skilled mechanic or an architect trains and develops, your relationship skills and mind-set need to follow a similar process. Through hands-on experiences, you gain information and knowledge to ensure your growth, and make changes in order to stabilize your shelf-life.

To give you an example, I will use my personal story to shed light on some of my own experiences in order to help you comprehend how I developed my toolbox over time and how I ultimately became **broken** being Too Cool To LOVE, then I will share some of the **tools** I used to **fix** it.

Growing up on the hard knock streets of Cleveland, Ohio, I faced the common challenge of not having a father present for most of my formative years. This unfortunate circumstance is a common narrative in too many families across the nation. And since this chapter uses tools as the metaphor, I compare my fatherless experience to being handed a broken pair of **pliers** to begin building my life.

Despite the absence of a male authority in the home, I was a bright, well-behaved adolescent that never missed a day of school, and was fortunate enough to experience love within the confines of my family environment. It was within those

Too Cool To LOVE

four walls that I witnessed the power of resilience and the importance of a family bond. My mother's love and dedication provided the basic framework for the foundation of my life, and for that, I consider myself lucky. I firmly believe that my early upbringing was a blessing, and that it laid the basic framework for my life's journey, which led me to you today.

Fast forward, I entered middle school, and my life experiences began to change. It was during this time that decisions became more challenging, as is true for most teenagers. Even back then peer pressure and societal influences pushed the agenda of determining one's "coolness" and acceptance.

My interest in girls began to surface, and as they noticed me too, I sought to make friends and impress them. I forged new friendships and, before long, found myself falling in love. I was head over heels for a girl at my school, and that marked the beginning of my journey down the Too Cool To LOVE path.

For weeks, we spent countless hours talking on the phone. She assured me that our love was mutual and that we would be together forever. I vividly recall walking her home one day, feeling nervous yet hopeful about that anticipated first kiss.

Unfortunately, I couldn't muster the courage needed, and the kiss never happened. To my dismay, the following week, I saw her leaving school early, hand-in-hand with an incredibly popular guy in the ninth grade. It shattered me. Deep down, I had a sinking feeling that they would eventually engage in a physical relationship.

Weeks later, she confirmed my fears and apologized for breaking my heart. When I questioned her about her choice, she explained that he was "super cool, fun, and more mature". Clearly, she was won over by his popularity and swag, and hearing those words devastated me.

It took many years for me to comprehend how that disappointment played a significant role in shaping my Too Cool To LOVE disposition. The combination of broken **pliers** and the painful **shears** pushed into my broken heart, formed a detrimental mix of emotional and physiological instability.

Consequently, those limited items in my toolbox shaped a **blueprint** that encouraged a lack of commitment and I started to build a string of emotionless relationships.

Based on the experience and the explanation from my first love, my desire to be more mature, which I understood to mean cooler and smoother, intensified. I yearned to grow up faster so that I could emulate the popular guy who had taken that first relationship prize from me. It was during this time that I began to pay closer attention to my older brother.

Among my older brothers, James stood out as the embodiment of the life I aspired to have one day. He was a prominent figure in our neighborhood, and I found myself drawn to him and his older friends. James, or as he was commonly known, Mac, possessed a responsible mindset even at a young age. At eighteen years old, he landed a high-paying job and quickly established himself as a hard worker who always pitched in to help mom. I deeply respected him and yearned to be just like him. Mac had it all—money, cars, the attention of women, and the respect of the entire neighborhood.

Both men and women admired him. He was the "Don" of that era, and I quickly realized that being his little brother came with certain built-in benefits, and a crown of "street credibility" was bestowed upon me.

All of his friends took me under their wings, and I was mentored like the young upcoming "Don." I became the neighborhood's little star, someone everyone wanted to protect, help, and groom for success.

At that age, the story sounded pretty good, and it was very exciting to be seen in this light. But, little did I know that during this time, I was adding some **gorilla glue** to my metaphorical toolbox, and I became firmly attached to tactics, games, and inappropriate behaviors that would harden my Too Cool To LOVE heart for decades.

Let me share with you a few examples of the tools my role models—Mac and his friends—gave me, or rather threw into my toolbox. And please remember, each tool added significant weight for me to carry around.

First, there was the **drill**. These young men drilled the **screws** of infidelity into me, and used **clamps** to seat me in the "player" high chair. I was encouraged to view relationships as mere games and to engage in multiple romantic pursuits without any sense of commitment or loyalty.

Then there was the **swiss knife**. They instilled in me the notion to have a stone-cold heart and warned against showing deep emotions, sensitivity, and to cut ties **(scissors)** with girls that wanted a commitment. It was all about maintaining an air of detachment and invulnerability.

And then there was the tool that was more like the **grenade**. Ok, this one might need some explaining. For this tool, the underlying concept was to pursue the most attractive and desirable women (the so-called dime pieces), but paradoxically, treat them as if they held very little value, as if they were at the bottom of the scale. The assignment was to undermine girls' self-esteem, gaining control over them and eventually taking full advantage of their emotional and psychological state of mind. This may sound perplexing or even disturbing, but within our group, it was believed that by standing out from everyone else who treated these girls (women) with adoration and respect, I would "subliminally" attract them and gain control over the relationship. The disturbing part is that as sick as it may sound, my tactics worked. But this tool was more dangerous than most, as the **shrapnel** of complete brokenness and low self-esteem kills everything in its path. Despite all the

Too Cool To LOVE

body bags around me, I simply stepped around them and continued down the dark road of Too Cool To LOVE.

During those formative years, I spent a significant amount of time with the boys in the hood at Robert Fulton Elementary school. It was our gathering spot, where we played basketball, hung out on the playground, and engaged in discussions about sexual conquests and more. I eagerly soaked it all in, oblivious to the impact it was having on me.

In those leisure moments, I became calibrated with the language and interpretation of derogatory terms such as "Bitches, Whores, Pimps, Players, and Hustlers." I didn't realize that those were the **measuring tape** and the **balance beam** used to perfectly position my nefarious mindset. My mental disposition was skewed, and I was transitioning from being a cleancut "mama's boy" to a cold-hearted player and somewhat of a pimp and a hustler.

As I moved along learning the **manual**, I unconsciously started using the **nails** and jagged pieces of **scrap metal** (lies and deceit) that were banging around in my toolbox. Oblivious to its noise, the sharp edges would cut me every time I reached inside to grab a tool to use. Eventually the blood would clot and turn into more hardened scars and calluses of numb emotions.

As I became fully immersed in this mindset, my grades suffered, and I started skipping school. I became caught up in the allure of the urban street culture, becoming mischievous, influential, and even engaging in criminal behaviors like breaking into houses. Fortunately, my first home invasion turned out to be a frivolous experience that I never repeated. Nonetheless, the act of having a thief's mindset did stain me because at that time I formed a reckless mindset for law and order, and this experience was like a **black marker** that I unconsciously carried around for years.

As you can see from the description, the hood mentality and methodologies had taken over me and I was a menace to society. The good news is that my mother was maternally intuitive and sensed the changes in me. In a surprising turn of events, she found me on the street corner, smoking a joint and gambling with dice for money. Mom shed a tear. Rather than responding with anger, yelling, or punishment, my mother silently drove us home. It was an unusual response that left a profound impact on me. However, the very next day, I found myself on an airplane bound for Los Angeles, California, to live with my father.

This bold move took my father by surprise, as mother hadn't informed him of my upcoming arrival until I was already in the air. She knew that her son was in danger amidst the perils of the urban streets and that I needed a strong male influence to guide me. She did not ask for my dad's consideration, discussion, or approval; she made the decision for my well-being—it was a swift and decisive action.

My dad, a devout Christian man who had remarried just six months prior, became my new guardian and mentor, and I became a new addition to his married life. I'm sure that unexpected responsibility was not an easy decision for any of my parents. But as the story continues, I found myself in a new place, a new environment, and I began developing a contrasting set of tools and behaviors for my toolbox.

My father swiftly transformed from merely being a dad to a true father figure, and I came to understand that there was a significant distinction between the two. Everything about Los Angeles and my new family was awe-inspiring. It was akin to the storyline of the Fresh Prince of Bel Air.

Unlike the hustlers, pimps, and players I encountered before, my father was the embodiment of respectability. His attire consisted of high-end suits, he lived in a nice home, driving only the best automobiles. What struck me the most was witnessing how he treated women with the utmost respect. He opened doors for his lady and always treated her as a high caliber woman, setting a new example for me.

In this contrasting environment and supported by my dad's influence, my toolbox began to undergo a transformation. The hustler-player mentality, and demeaning treatment of women were gradually replaced with a different set of tools. I now had tools that emphasized respect, honor, and the power of positive communication.

Under my dad's guidance, I also learned the power of the tongue, understanding that words could change or influence outcomes. This newfound understanding gave me **razor** sharp control of conversation, and this immediately became a tremendously powerful asset and tool.

Oh, and I should probably mention that my father is a pastor (yep, I'm a PK). My life quickly became all about church, church, and more church, which, in the long run, proved to be a beneficial factor for me. I was back on the straight and narrow path, living an honest life. I was witnessing firsthand what a healthy marital relationship looked like and how a good man should interact with his family and community.

At fifteen years old, I enrolled at Dorsey High School for my freshman year, eager to embark on this new chapter of my life.

The Maclin family thrived, and I had an abundance of positive experiences to draw from in a prosperous, God-fearing home. As I reflect on those formative years, again, I must acknowledge that I was very fortunate to have additional stable illustrations and positive images to draw from.

However, even within this more grounded environment, it became a bit awkward for me to navigate high school as a devout Christian. I still had a strong desire to be cool and fit in with my fellow high school students.

Fortunately, my streak of good fortune continued, and I managed to become part of the most popular clique in school, known as "The MBs.", the Mysterious Brothers. I forged a friendship with the leader of the group, which was a significant achievement because he was truly impressive. He possessed good looks, popularity, and a high level of street credibility and respect. To me, he was the "Don" of Dorsey High School, and the epitome of a player. I deeply admired him.

I began mirroring and rekindling some of the thoughts and habits from my Ohio-based toolbox. Little did I know that both the EAST and West coast had similar forms of operation. They both mirrored the hustler mentality, being a player, and treating an attractive girl like she was nothing, these were widespread misguided notions.

But the games and erroneous behaviors grew even more intense in Los Angeles. My crew exuded boldness, a high fashion sense, and popularity. We had many girls interested in us, leading to numerous dating and relationship experiences. However, in the MB crew, anyone who dared to express sincere feelings for a girl or desired to have a committed relationship was singled out, mocked, and clowned. We relentlessly attacked them, ensuring they felt uncomfortable even considering such notions.

It was like emotions and commitment were unheard of phenomenons, and anyone who expressed them was referred to as a "Sucka Duck". If any one of us showed any signs of falling in love, the other crew members would aggressively slap a big (S) on the perpetrators chest, effectively branding them as a punk, a sucker, a sissy, someone soft. In our crew, breaking the players' code by displaying genuine emotions, forming deep connections, or expressing love and caring for a girl was considered feeble and weak.

This frat-like group maintained a black box with a big red **velcro "S"** symbol inside. We deliberately chose the color red and reacted as if it were an **emergency shut off button**. If anyone persisted in their emotional expressions, the crew would cease all their interactions and activities, and not allow them to hang with us until they stopped showing any signs of emotional weakness. We revelled in exposing and shaming any crew member who dared to suggest they were falling in love. At the time, it seemed like harmless high school banter and fun. Looking back, I now understand the lasting and cruel impact of those actions.

None of the MB's realized that we were cultivating a sense of infidelity, numbness, and emotional disconnection. That frat Sucka Duck mindset ingrained a deeply rooted negative association with relationship commitment for all of us. Subliminally, we discarded any remnants of love or affection from our toolboxes. The **vise grip wrench** needed to securely lock onto such emotions was absent in our group.

But at that time, who knew? I felt like I was at the pinnacle of sexiness. I had assimilated the language of the bi-coastal pimp and hustler game, sprinkled on top of that was spiritual knowledge and my power with razor sharp words. My ability to articulate and get what I wanted had become a potent and wicked gift.

I had the crew, the girls, high-school fame (so to speak), and life seemed epic. At least, that's what I thought at the time. Today, my truth is different. I was a complete mess. I believed that it was sexy, fun, and cool, but in reality, it wasn't. Especially not according to the transformed person I am today.

The purpose of me sharing my rollercoaster coaster life experiences, and history is to help you understand what prepared and programmed me to become Too Cool To LOVE, and how by the time I reached my mid-to-late twenties, my toolbox was filled with inadequate tools and tainted ideologies about women and relationships. And how I found myself exhausted and confused because deep in my heart, I truly desired a soulmate.

I had matured enough to know that I wanted to share a meaningful, Eros relationship, with someone special and to start a family. But it was like I had a bag of dry **cement**, but no **water** to mix in order to create the foundation. I lacked the proper tools and enough experience to accomplish the task. It was like trying to move the **sandpaper** of my life with a **crane**. And even though I knew how to get on the boat of love and opportunity, I certainly didn't know how to catch and keep a woman's attention. I was still hitting way too hard with my **hammer**. Inadvertently, I kept damaging everything around me and sunk every ship I stepped on. Like many of you, I was using the wrong tools, and not properly trained or qualified for a healthy, balanced relationship.

Now that you get the gist of my Too Cool to LOVE upbringing. I encourage you to use it as an example and look back at your own life history, and conduct a review of those formative years. It can be a valuable tool to help you understand where you are today. Identify past experiences that contributed to the creation of harmful tools that may be holding you back from establishing quality relationships. Determine which tools need to be replaced or recalibrated. In some cases, you may need to PURGE them altogether.

I acknowledge that my toolbox story may appear cute and light in nature. However, some of you may have endured severely abusive and tormenting developmental and/or adult years, which can leave emotional scars and deeply affect your psychological well-being. If that is the case, it may be challenging to take a hard look back and delve into those painful experiences known as the **paint brushes** of your life – left as dry, brittle fibers of emotions in your toolbox. In such instances, I sincerely recommend seeking the help of a good mentor or professional therapist who can guide you through these turbulent waters, hopefully without resorting to medication. It may require more effort to find the silver lining, but it is crucial and will add tremendous value once you discover and deal with your truth.

The truth is, in order to be ready for a new relationship or repair existing ones, you need a proper set of clean, recalibrated tools and a sturdy toolbox. And you can begin to refill it with the tools of self-love, self-acceptance, and all the other

Too Cool To LOVE

items that you will find in the Too Cool To LOVE chapters ahead.

Remember, your toolbox is not set in stone. It is dynamic and can be continually improved and refined. With the right tools and a commitment to self-improvement, you can transform your relationship with yourself, and others to create a life filled with love, peace and happiness.

Thanks for digging into my tool box with me. Now it is time to sift through yours, and embark on the journey of becoming free from the Too Cool To LOVE matrix.

6
Life's Too Short:
Too Cool To Save Time

TIME
Its movement is essential
It plays favorites for no one
to conquer love
or to be revengeful
Time pushes us to the end.

The above is a short poem I wrote when I was nineteen years old. Over the years it often circled around my brain, but I never knew what its purpose was until this moment in my life.

As a part of this book, and your journey, I'm obligated to let you know that TIME is not playing or wasting even a second of your life or those around you.

What that means in terms of your life is that you must take time seriously before your time ends. It is unbelievable how one day you are twenty-five years old, and a few memories later, your fifty-year-old face is staring back at you in the mirror, wondering where the time went.

The billion-dollar question is, at what point will you look at what is important for your life and establish the fundamental behaviors to achieve the goals that are most important to you?

Once you firmly establish this, you can then set the pace for your life, and set standards for others who want to be in it. These people will either make a deposit of positive influence, or create a negative deficit. In either case you have to account for the time, and it is imperative that you insist on time with a positive return on your life investment.

Since this entire book is about establishing love for yourself, and perhaps with others, you should savor as much time as you can. The problem with "Too Cool To LOVE" people and behavior is that they often don't factor in time, so they waste theirs and yours. Trust me, you do not need or want to sacrifice time in any area of your life, especially not your love life.

Remember, you control the ticks of your clock. Life is much too short to let others cause any level of imbalance in your life. Time is wasted when we walk around sad, sour, or sorry about our existence or any past hard-knock experiences. Whatever the past experiences were, you are here today with the power to overcome them and take back your time.

Too Cool To LOVE

Find your passion, identify your dreams early, and go after them. Visualize your world filled with personal, professional, and financial accomplishments. See yourself having an abundance of love and support. You should be traveling the world and experiencing all the wonderment this earth has to offer. Time and life are short, and you should live like you appreciate the sun, oxygen, air, and wind while time provides them for you.

Truth is, it is simple. Just be yourself. Be honest, true, and live within all that encompasses a roadmap of fulfillment for you. Anything less than that is unacceptable.

Top 40 list of statements to make and actions to take:

- 1. Life is too short to waste on pretending to be someone you're not. Embrace your authenticity and let your true self shine.

- 2. Don't spend a moment living a lie when life is too short to deny your innermost desires and passions.

- 3. Life is fleeting, so seize every opportunity to live your purpose, for tomorrow may never come.

- 4. Embrace your uniqueness, for life is too short to conform to someone else's expectations.

- 5. Time is precious, don't squander it on pursuits that don't align with your true calling.

- 6. Life's brevity demands that you pursue your dreams relentlessly and fearlessly.

- 7. Don't let the sands of time slip through your fingers; make every moment count living your truth.

- 8. Life is too short to be held captive by others' opinions; liberate yourself and live authentically.

- 9. Embrace your passions with fervor, for life's transience reminds us that hesitation is a waste.

- 10. Don't let fear rob you of the chance to live your truth to the fullest. Embrace life boldly.

- 11. Life's clock is ticking, don't wait for the "perfect" moment to start living in your purpose.

- 12. Celebrate your uniqueness, for life is too short to conform to societal norms.

- 13. Time is a fleeting gift; spend it wisely, nourishing your soul with meaningful pursuits.

- 14. Life is too short to stay confined in the cocoon of doubt. Take flight and embrace your true self.

- 15. Don't let the passing seconds go to waste; use them to create a life that aligns with your values.

- 16. Embrace your journey wholeheartedly, for life's brevity reminds us to cherish every step.

- 17. Life is too short to let others dictate your path. Take charge of your destiny and follow your heart.

- 18. Time waits for no one; don't let the fear of judgment hold you back from living your truth.

- 19. Don't let the sands of time bury your dreams. Pursue your passions relentlessly.

- 20. Life's ephemerality reminds us to cherish every moment, living with purpose and authenticity.

- 21. Surround yourself with kindred souls; life is too short to let toxic influences drain your energy.

- 22. Time is precious, don't allow others to waste it for you. Set boundaries and protect your moments.

- 23. Embrace those who uplift your spirit; life is too short to be weighed down by negative energy.

- 24. Be selective with your time and invest it in people who share your values and lift you higher.

- 25. Life is too short to entertain relationships that don't align with your vision and purpose.

- 26. Surround yourself with like-minded individuals who inspire and challenge you to grow.

- 27. Time is irreplaceable; spend it with those who appreciate and cherish your authentic self.

- 28. Don't let others drain your energy; life is too short to have people who don't value you in your inner circle.

- 29. Life's brevity reminds us to prioritize relationships that nourish our souls and bring joy.

- 30. Embrace the company of those who support your journey and celebrate your unique path.

- 31. Time is a finite resource; spend it on relationships that add value and meaning to your life.

- 32. Don't waste precious moments seeking approval from those who don't share your values.

- 33. Life is too short to be dragged down by negative influences. Surround yourself with positivity.

- 34. Time is a non-renewable asset; don't let others monopolize it with their negativity.

- 35. Invest your time wisely in people who contribute to your growth and happiness.

- 36. Life's brevity demands that you cherish every moment and spend it with those who truly matter.

- 37. Don't compromise your values to fit in with others; life is too short to live a counterfeit existence.

- 38. Time is your most precious currency; invest it in relationships that nourish your soul.

- 39. Surround yourself with those who appreciate your authenticity and encourage your dreams.

- 40. Life is too short to have people in your life who don't respect and honor your truth.

Too Cool To LOVE

Remember, life is a fleeting gift, and every moment counts. Live your truth, embrace your purpose, and surround yourself with people who uplift and inspire you on your journey.

7
The Trophy Life:
Too Cool To Know True Value

Ah, the allure of the good life, where opulence reigns, and one is surrounded by the finest luxuries that this world has to offer. On the perfectly sculpted marble mantelpiece of your mansion, sits a platinum trophy declaring, "I Go For Mine, Cause I Got To Shine."

Let's be clear, trophies and awards are undeniably uplifting, representing triumphs over challenges, achievements, and success in various aspects of life, be it academics, sports, or personal accomplishments. Embracing and celebrating such accolades is entirely justified.

Yet, in this chapter, we will focus on the potential pitfalls and hazards associated with pursuing relationship trophies. All too often, people chase after partners who are visually appealing or coveted for the admiration they attract from others. However, basing a relationship solely on superficial aspects can be perilous and jeopardize the possibility of long-term, meaningful connections. The trophy life, if fixated upon without caution, can lead to dissatisfaction and leave you entrapped in a never-ending maze of shallow desires.

To build a truly fulfilling and sustainable relationship, we must look beyond the surface and embrace the essential elements that form the foundation of a genuine connection. It is essential to recognize that true love and lasting companionship are nurtured by qualities such as understanding, communication, shared values, and emotional intimacy. While the thrill of possessing a trophy partner may be intoxicating, it seldom sustains a profound and meaningful bond.

Instead of being dazzled by external attributes, let us focus on cultivating a deeper understanding of ourselves and our partners. Seeking a soulmate who complements us, understands our values, and contributes to our growth will lead us to a fulfilling and enduring relationship. The trophy life may appear glamorous, but it is the beauty of genuine love and connection that truly enriches our lives.

As I began to write this chapter, I made a bold decision to leave my home in Los Angeles, CA, and escape from my base of cultural behaviors that challenges my growth to this day.

One of the major issues that permeates The Trophy Life is what many know as "THE SCALE."

The scale is a common practice that many of us use as a rating system to evaluate potential partners. This socially accepted grading component has become a significant problem for both men and women seeking meaningful relationships.

Breaking free from this societal norm is an ongoing process, and I admit that I, too, struggle with The Scale at times. Admittedly, it's one of the key reasons I have been single for years. Unlike some authors and relationship coaches who speak from a successful marriage track record, my perspective comes from being "Too Cool" like many of you.

My mission is to help us evolve beyond the superficial tactics and behaviors that hinder us from experiencing true love. This includes the mindset associated with the world-renowned trophy life, which represents the top-shelf, idealized vision of happiness we often chase.

Our society constantly bombards us with images of abundance and high society, pushing us to look, feel, and live in a certain way. These messages become ingrained in our consciousness, leading us to desire the illustrious trophy life promoted by luxurious brands. And with social media now an integral part of our lives, the pressure for instant gratification and the urge to showcase our achievements only intensify the problem.

Social media and the well-branded Trophy Life perpetuate an alternative plot, hooking us for life with unrealistic expectations and a fixation on quick fixes and instant gratification. As social platforms continue to evolve, we must remain vigilant and recalibrate our perspectives to avoid falling into these traps.

The key is to prioritize genuine connections and meaningful values over superficial appearances and societal expectations. Embracing self-love and authenticity is a crucial step towards breaking free from the allure of the trophy life. By pushing back against these societal pressures and redefining our pursuit of happiness, we can find fulfillment in real, sustainable relationships that go beyond the glossy exterior.

The Trophy Life (Men)

In the quest for the trophy life, men often prioritize having the most beautiful woman by their side to showcase and boast about - the coveted "dime piece." Let's face it; many men relish the compliments they receive when people admire their attractive partner. It becomes a means of feeding their egos, turning each moment into a triumph to be exploited.

But beneath this pursuit are crucial questions that remain concealed: how happy are they truly? Is the woman they seek merely a captivating sight, or does she bring a sense of purpose and ministry to their lives? Can she be a reliable partner, even in the face of adversity, like being a "wheelchair pusher"? There's nothing inherently wrong with being drawn to a physically appealing partner, as long as the foundation of the relationship is grounded in substance and sustenance - and yes, that's entirely possible.

However, it's disheartening how often I receive phone calls or engage in conversations with men fixated on numeric ratings like "I met a 9.4 last night," referring to the infamous scale.

They become enamored with a woman's physical attractiveness, obsessing over her appearance from head to toe, yet often overlooking crucial aspects such as her character, background, and values. Men will often tolerate various frivolous behaviors for the sake of possessing a so-called trophy piece.

While physical attraction is undoubtedly a natural aspect of human relationships, grading or embracing a woman solely based on aesthetics sets the stage for failure. This mindset leads to relationship pitfalls that many men with such shallow thinking are bound to encounter.

Moreover, it's important to consider that these so-called dime pieces may carry emotional and psychological instabilities from their childhood and past dating experiences. Their constant objectification and being gawked since childhood, may likely contribute to deep-rooted imbalances. And let's be clear, women with the dime piece disposition often seek a man who can provide them with the trophy life they envision, someone who can support their desires for a lavish lifestyle, not yours.

To be fair, not all physically attractive women are driven by this high-scale mindset. However, for those who do possess such skewed perspectives, they are well aware that men desire arm candy. They believe, "If I'm going to be arm candy, why settle for a shoemaker, a bank teller, or a grocery store manager?" Sometimes, even a decent six-figure income won't suffice for the extravagant lifestyle these types of women crave. And let's be honest; most men cannot afford to maintain the level of opulence they desire.

Eventually, many men find themselves feeling the pressure and heat that comes with the pursuit of a trophy partner. The perceived solution for some is to venture out of the country to places like Brazil, Ethiopia, or Thailand, where it seems easier to attract and retain women. However, this belief is a myth, a "man-code" misconception. The economic differences and financial challenges might make it appear easier, but it's not a sustainable or healthy approach. Essentially, in such cases, the men (consciously or unconsciously) end up putting these women on a retainer and exploiting them, and basically treating them as a "work for hire" trophy.

While foreign women often make the men feel like a King, there's often an imbalance between their lives and cultures. These women are not viewed as long-term life partners but rather collector's items, or trophies, and they cannot be hidden forever. Once they are exposed to the world of luxury and other opportunities, their desires and horizons may expand, and they may move on to the next best thing, you guessed it, The Trophy Life, a bigger, better trophy. The traps and desires of trophy life can be relentless, and it's essential for men to understand what they need to do in order to break free from this cycle.

Ultimately, it requires inner work to shift one's mindset and align oneself with a higher state of self-belief and purpose. When a man is operating at this level of self-awareness and has his life together, he becomes capable of attracting the right people for his life and creating meaningful relationships.

The Trophy Life (Women)

Now, let's explore the trophy life from the perspective of women. It becomes evident that their focus is vastly different. While they would appreciate a man who is strong and handsome, their primary intent often revolves around finding a partner with a "healthy lifetime" wallet. They certainly prefer to boast to their girlfriends about the luxurious experiences they enjoy with their wealthy partners, such as being picked up in a Bentley, dining at Michelin five-star restaurants, and traveling to exotic destinations. Financial security and the ability to flaunt their partner's wealth take precedence over other aspects, such as physical appearance.

This focus on wealth and luxury may even lead some women to overlook certain criteria or qualities they would typically desire in a partner. The allure of living the carefree life of luxury becomes so enticing that they may neglect important sensibilities, such as properly caring for their provider or seeking true compatibility. In their pursuit of the trophy life, they may sacrifice deeper connections and meaningful relationships.

It's fascinating to note that some of the most stunning women end up with less conventionally attractive men. This might be because their ultimate goal is to secure financial stability and wealth rather than seeking a balanced and fulfilling relationnship. They are willing to forego their rigid lists of partner criteria for a chance to live what they consider to be the trophy life, a life filled with luxury and the display of prestigious possessions.

However, this pursuit of trophy life can be a double-edged sword. While it offers glimpses of a glamorous lifestyle, it might not lead to genuine happiness and fulfillment in the long run. As with men, it's crucial for women to reconsider their priorities and values when it comes to relationships, focusing on what truly matters for a sustainable and rewarding union.

In the pursuit of the trophy life, women must be reminded that men of power and wealth may offer material comforts, but they do not guarantee happiness. Wealthy individuals often have a certain lifestyle and social circle, and they may treat the trophy piece as a temporary companion, showering her with gifts and attention, but not committing to a long-term relationship. And in many cases, they may already have a more stable partner back home whom they fully commit to.

At a younger age, it might seem easy to dream of finding a wealthy and successful partner. As time goes on, however, the reality sets in that the big commitment or marriage contract from a high-profile executive or celebrity may not materialize. The years pass, and while you remain attractive and accomplished, finding "Mr. Right" becomes increasingly challenging.

Women may try to enhance their attractiveness by pursuing education and self-improvement, realizing that being a pretty face alone may not be enough to win the heart of someone with substantial means. While education is a valuable asset that can provide stability and self-sufficiency, and is an important milestone, it does not ensure that you will land a wealthy partner.

The pursuit of financial dreams can lead to pitfalls. Many so-called pretty girls may get involved with the wrong crowd, such as street cats, drug dealers, or predatory individuals, seeking a taste of the luxurious lifestyle they desire. However, this path often ends in disaster. Street hustlers may offer a taste of the trophy life, but they rarely lead to a stable and fulfilling relationship. Instead, they often lead to abuse or other forms of trouble, such as them ending up in jail, dead, or broke.

While some might be inspired by rags-to-riches stories like Jay Z's, it is essential to acknowledge that very few people achieve such extraordinary success. Chasing a fantasy lifestyle through risky means can have severe consequences and derail the pursuit of a fulfilling and lasting relationship. It is vital to be cautious and avoid sacrificing one's well-being for the allure of the trophy life.

A Trophy Life Message for All:

In the pursuit of a trophy life, one of the significant challenges we face is the passage of time. How much of our lives are we willing to invest in waiting until we attain everything on our checklist? How many potential partners do we dismiss because they don't measure up to the standards set by our scales?

We may have encountered great potential relationship partners along the way – the entrepreneur, bank teller, or delivery driver – but our obsession with the trophy life often hinders us from seeing their true worth. We wear the "Too Cool" shades that blind us to genuine connections, potentially missing out on fulfilling relationships.

However, this fixation on wealth can lead to compromises for all genders, and they may find themselves stuck in unsatisfying situations as mere "order takers" to their partners.
The underlying message is that we need to break free from these traps that keep us confined to the illusion of the trophy life. It is essential to recognize that there's nothing inherently wrong with aspiring for a high-end lifestyle, but we must reevaluate our priorities and mindset when it comes to seeking meaningful relationships.

Let's recalibrate and shift our focus away from superficial attributes. The key to genuine happiness lies in finding someone who is compatible and reliable, someone who brings balance, purpose, and ministry to our lives. That's the true 10 on "The Scale". These core elements are the foundation of true peace and happiness, outweighing looks or wealth.

If both men and women focus on fostering balance, support, and mutual growth within a relationship, they may find that they can build a partnership with extraordinary potential, and create a billion-dollar venture. That said, it is crucial to avoid making relationships solely about monetary benefits or external success. When the connection is based on genuine values, compatibility, and a shared sense of purpose, the peace within the relationship becomes invaluable.

Ultimately, we need to change our mindset and break free from the addiction of chasing trophies. By recognizing the true value of a partner and embracing compatibility and reliability as the ultimate metrics, we can pursue a good life, and find lasting happiness in our relationships.

By releasing the obsession with appearances and material wealth, we open ourselves up to the possibility of attracting a love that goes beyond fleeting external factors. Instead, we strive to build relationships on solid foundations, much like the enduring monuments of ancient civilizations. These relics are sturdy, strong, and resilient, capable of weathering the test of time.

Developing and nurturing core values within ourselves is the crucial step. Prioritizing self-fulfillment and self-sufficiency allows us to be whole individuals who are not dependent on others for our happiness. Only when we have established this solid core can we attract and develop relationships that genuinely add value to our lives.

Let's be clear: omitting the superficial specifics of looks or wealth does not mean settling for less. Everyone has desires and preferences, but it's vital to discern between what truly matters and what is merely a societal construct. Rather than pursuing the illusion of the "Trophy Life," we should strive to become the trophy ourselves – individuals who radiate authenticity, compassion, and emotional depth.

Too Cool To LOVE

In this pursuit of authentic connections, remember that everyone can be a trophy, and everyone should have a trophy life – one filled with love, joy, and contentment. However, it's crucial to navigate the path with caution and choose the right tools to achieve this meaningful connection.

By embracing this life stance, you are demonstrating courage and self-awareness, taking a step towards mastering the art of genuine, lasting love. Embrace the principles of self-love, and in doing so, you will attract the best that life has to offer.

Keep your heart and eyes fixed on the person who genuinely loves and accepts you for who you are. Avoid chasing after those who require flashy goods or material allure to be convinced of your worth. True love goes beyond external facades; it lies in the connection of hearts and souls, bound by mutual respect and admiration.

So, go forth with confidence and an open heart, knowing that the best is yet to come on this beautiful journey of love and self-discovery. Remember the wisdom in cherishing and nurturing genuine connections – that is the true essence of the Trophy Life.

Too Cool To LOVE

Footnote:

"Keep your heart and eyes fixed on the person that has shown their commitment to love you for you. The one you have to chase or use flashy goods to convince is likely not the one."

The Trophy Life in quick review:

"The Trophy Life (Men)"

- "Let's be honest, every man loves the 'dime piece,' but happiness goes beyond appearances."

- "Chasing after physical attractiveness can lead to relationship failures if it lacks sustenance."

- "Factor in emotional and physiological instabilities that often come with high-scale mindset women."

- "Overlooking important qualities for the sake of a trophy piece can be a risky endeavor."

- "Going abroad to find easier conquests might result in a short-lived, superficial relationship."

- "A trophy piece may provide short-term validation but lacks the substance for a lasting connection."

- "Realize that self-belief and a balanced life ministry attract the right people into your life."

"The Trophy Life (Women)"

- "Seeking financial security shouldn't overshadow the importance of finding genuine happiness."

- "Attracting wealth doesn't guarantee a committed and loving partner."

- "People of wealth seek more than just looks; education and self-sustainability hold value."

- "Be cautious of attracting the wrong type of partners while pursuing the financial dream."

- "Beware of getting involved with street hustlers, as their lifestyle often ends in tragic consequences."

- "Open yourself to a life companion willing to support and balance your aspirations."

- "Riding on a high horse of unrealistic expectations may hinder your chances of finding true love."

Break time: Here is where you should take my suggestion to pause and recalibrate your thoughts as more mandatory. The next few chapters ahead

Too Cool To LOVE

are heavy and will walk you through some dark times and perhaps be difficult in nature.

So before moving on, go to the TooCoolToLove playlist on Spotify and listen to "The Good Life" by Kanye West and T Pain. The song will motivate you and perhaps cause you to acknowledge and accept the good things about the good life. Play the song a few times before moving on.

8
WTF:
Too Cool To Unravel It

Take a deep breath and brace yourself because we're about to dive into the perplexing world of modern relationship culture. It's a world that often leaves us exclaiming, "WTF" Though we'll refrain from using an abundance of explicit language, the sentiment behind it remains: What The F--- is going on?

In this chapter, I will aim to unravel the complex web of expectations, demands, and confusion that plague today's dating and relationship landscape. I understand that you're tired of trying to keep up, exhausted by the ever-changing rules, and frustrated by the seemingly unattainable standards set by society. Well, you are not alone.

Picture yourself standing amidst a swirling storm of relationship chaos, a tornado fueled by social media, romanticized ideals, and a constant stream of mixed signals. You find yourself questioning your own worth and struggling to navigate the turbulent waters of love and connection. It's enough to make anyone want to throw their hands up in defeat and scream, "WTF!"

The truth is, the modern relationship culture has become a labyrinth of contradictions. On one hand, we're told to be independent, self-sufficient individuals who don't need anyone else to complete us. On the other hand, we're bombarded with images of picture-perfect couples, extravagant gestures of love, and an idealized version of romance that seems unattainable. The dating terrain has transformed into a fast-paced game of swipes, likes, and superficial connections. It's become a numbers game, where the quantity of matches and virtual interactions outweighs the quality of genuine human connection. It's no wonder you're feeling overwhelmed and disillusioned.

In an effort to remove the debris and clear a path, let's shine a light on a few basic examples that highlight the perplexing dynamics of modern dating and relationships, leaving both men and women wondering, "WTF is going on?"

One prevalent scenario that can leave us scratching our heads is when women head out to social settings with the expectation that someone will foot the bill for their drinks or provide bottle service all night. In some cases, when a group of women gathers, there may be an unspoken assumption that they can enjoy a top-shelf evening without investing any of their own resources. While it's not inherently wrong to be treated or to enjoy the company of others, the issue arises when this expectation becomes the norm, and entitlement takes precedence over personal responsibility.

On the other side of the coin, men sometimes fall into the trap of expecting intimacy or sexual favors in return for their efforts and financial investments. Taking a woman out for drinks, dinner, or engaging in various activities should not automatically entitle a man to access a woman's most private space. It's crucial to recognize that consent, boundaries, and mutual desire are essential components of any intimate relationship.

Assuming that financial investments alone warrant physical intimacy not only undermines the concept of consent but also perpetuates an unhealthy power dynamic.

This mindset and type of social behavior foster an unsound sense of rights and prerogatives, and establishes a license for today's dating culture to operate in an atmosphere of transactional interactions.

It seems as though we have huddled up on a relationship playing field where genuine connection and mutual respect take a backseat to expensive outings and elaborate gifts, and those have become "the relationship barometer". And W(when)TF did that become ok?

And it may be important to note, that ultimately no one wins the fun-on-the-run, entitlement game. So the only realities left to pan out are, who will use whom the most during the transaction period, and when time and age catch up with you, will there be enough left of you to ultimately find and offer true love?

Another key issue plaguing modern dating is the diminishing presence of gratitude and appreciation. In the past, expressing gratitude for kind gestures and showing appreciation for someone's efforts were seen as fundamental aspects of building meaningful connections. However, in today's fast-paced and self-centered society, these virtues have become less prevalent.

And WTF is happening to chivalry? Chivalry, once revered as a sign of respect, honor, and admiration towards women, seems to have faded into obscurity. Many men no longer embrace the principles of chivalry, and perhaps more perplexing is that some women no longer appreciate or desire it. This shift in mental disposition has further fueled the disconnection between the sexes.

So, WTF is going on? Part of the answer lies in the changing dynamics of gender roles and societal expectations. As gender norms evolve, traditional ideas of chivalry may be seen as outdated or even patronizing to some women. Men, on the other hand, may feel uncertain about how to navigate this shifting landscape and may choose to avoid chivalrous acts altogether.

The rise of individualism and self-centeredness has also played a significant role in the erosion of basic values. The pursuit of personal success and gratification has taken precedence over fostering meaningful connections and practicing gratitude. As a result, acts of kindness, consideration, and respect have been relegated to the sidelines. Yes, there is a lot going on, and these items are just the tip of the iceberg.

Too Cool To LOVE

It is my strong opinion that it's time, and necessary to reevaluate and repurpose our thinking. Both men and women must strive for genuine connections based on mutual respect, equality, and shared values. It's essential to move away from transactional thinking and focus on building authentic relationships where individuals contribute based on their own capacity and desire, rather than expecting entitlement or taking advantage of others.

By embracing open communication, establishing clear boundaries, and advocating for a culture of respect, we can move toward healthier and more fulfilling relationships. It's time to let go of psychological notions of entitlement and focus on building connections based on mutual understanding, trust, and shared experiences.

In order to unravel these debilitating chains, we must first challenge the status quo. We need to question the narratives that have been fed to us, the false ideals that have been ingrained in our minds, and the unrealistic expectations that have been placed upon us. It's time to reclaim our agency and define our own version of happiness and fulfillment. Instead of striving for perfection or seeking validation from others, let's focus on building genuine connections based on mutual respect, trust, and shared values. Let's prioritize emotional well-being, self-love, and personal growth. It's time to shift our perspective from external validation to internal fulfillment.

WTF (WHY)

As we look deeper into the intricacies of today's relationship culture, it becomes crucial to explore the question of why things have become so challenging and, for many, even depressing. And why the fundamental principles of good old-fashioned manners, patience, and respect seem to be overshadowed and all but lost in the chaos of modern dating and relationships.

One of the key factors contributing to the WTF agony is the rapid advancement of technology and the rise of social media. In an era where instant gratification and superficial connections prevail, genuine human interaction and meaningful connections have taken a backseat. The ease of swiping left or right, the constant bombardment of options, and the never ending pursuit of the next best thing have created a disposable mindset when it comes to relationships.

Moreover, the normalization of hookup culture has blurred the lines between casual encounters and genuine emotional connections. The emphasis on physicality and immediate pleasure often overshadows the importance of emotional intimacy and long-term commitment. People have become conditioned to expect quick fixes and instant validation, leaving little room for the slow-burning fires of genuine love and understanding to ignite.

Another contributing factor is the fear of vulnerability. In a world where everyone seems to be curating their lives for social media, there is an underlying pressure to project an image of perfection and flawlessness. The fear of being judged or rejected for one's true self has led to the construction of carefully crafted personas, making it challenging to build authentic connections. The Too Cool To LOVE masks we wear to protect ourselves end up becoming barriers that hinder genuine intimacy and prevent us from truly knowing and being known by another person.

Additionally, the ever-increasing pace of life, career demands, and societal pressures have left little time for nurturing relationships. People are constantly juggling multiple responsibilities, chasing success, and striving to meet societal expectations. This frenetic pace often leaves individuals exhausted, emotionally unavailable, and unable to invest the time and effort required to build meaningful connections. The result is a culture that prioritizes convenience over depth, leaving many feeling unfulfilled and disconnected.

Furthermore, the prevalence of ghosting, breadcrumbing, and other forms of emotional manipulation has become all too common. The lack of communication and accounta-bility in today's dating landscape can leave individuals feeling bewildered, hurt, and questioning their self-worth. The uncertainty and unpredictability of these interactions can take a toll on one's mental and emotional well-being, leading to a pervasive sense of confusion and frustration.

In essence, the WTF nature of today's relationship culture stems from a combination of factors: the influence of technology and social media, the normalization of hookup culture, the fear of vulnerability, the fast-paced nature of modern life, and the prevalence of emotional manipulation. Understanding these underlying dynamics can help us navigate this complex landscape with more clarity and intention.

WTF (WHEN)

In the midst of the chaotic and confusing landscape of modern relationships, it's natural to find yourself wondering, "When" will it be over?" When will we break free from the clutches of the current dating nightmares, and find the peace and fulfillment we yearn for? In this final section of the WTF chapter, we'll explore some new and fresh ideas that can pave the way for positive change and liberation from the challenges of today's relationship culture.

Now that we have examined the perplexing nature of today's relationship culture and determined some reasons behind its WTF essence, it's time to redirect our energies to finding the answers. While navigating the challenges and frustrations of modern relationships may seem daunting, there are strategies and approaches that can help us reclaim our power and create fulfilling connections.

The steps and information below will help you explore specific tools and techniques to enhance your relationship skills and create a solid foundation for long-term, meaningful connections. Get ready to move further into the realm of self-growth and relationship mastery.

Self-Reflection and Awareness:

The journey begins with looking inward and gaining a deeper understanding of yourself. Take the time to reflect on your values, needs, and aspirations in relationships. What are your non-negotiables? What do you truly desire in a partner? By knowing yourself better, you can set clear intentions and make conscious choices that align with your authentic self.

Setting Boundaries:

Establishing healthy boundaries is crucial to maintaining self-respect and fostering healthy relationships. You must clearly communicate your boundaries and expectations to potential partners and be willing to enforce them. Remember that you deserve to be treated with kindness, respect, and consideration.

Authenticity and Vulnerability:

Embrace your true self and allow yourself to be vulnerable. Genuine connections are built on honesty, openness, and the willingness to show up as your authentic self. By letting go of masks and pretenses, you create space for deeper connections based on mutual understanding and acceptance.

Mindful Communication:

Foster effective and compassionate communication in your relationships. Practice active listening, empathy, and non-judgment. Communicate your feelings, needs, and concerns openly and honestly, whilst also being receptive to your partner's perspective. Healthy communication forms the foundation for trust and intimacy.

Prioritizing Emotional Well-being:

Take care of your emotional well-being and prioritize self-care. Engage in activities that bring you joy, practice self-compassion, and cultivate a support network of friends and loved ones. Recognize when a relationship is causing emotional harm or draining your energy and be willing to let go if necessary.

Mindful Dating:

Approach dating with a mindful and intentional mindset. Rather than swiping through profiles mindlessly, take the time to get to know potential partners on a deeper level. Look beyond surface-level qualities and consider compatibility in values, goals, and lifestyles. Slow down the process and allow connections to develop naturally.

Practicing Emotional Intelligence:

In the quest to end the dating nightmare, developing emotional intelligence is crucial. This involves cultivating self-awareness, recognizing and managing our own emotions and having an empathetic understanding of the emotions of others. By honing these skills, we can navigate conflicts more effectively, communicate our needs clearly, and build deeper connections based on emotional understanding and support.

Mindful Technology Usage:

In today's digital age, technology plays a significant role in our relationships. However, it's important to use technology mindfully and consciously. Rather than relying solely on dating apps or social media for connection, we should strive for a healthy balance between virtual interactions and face-to-face experiences. Being present in the moment, setting boundaries around technology use, and prioritizing genuine human connection can help restore authenticity and depth to our relationships.

Cultivating Patience and Acceptance:

In a fast-paced world, cultivating patience and acceptance is crucial for finding lasting love. Rome wasn't built in a day, and neither are meaningful relationships. It's essential to allow the natural progression of a connection, avoiding the urge to rush or force things. Additionally, practicing acceptance means embracing the imperfections and quirks of ourselves and our partners. By fostering patience and acceptance, we create space for growth, understanding, and authentic connection to flourish.

Engaging in Self-Reflection:

To break free from the dating nightmare, self-reflection is vital. Taking the time to assess our own desires, beliefs, and patterns can lead to profound insights and personal growth. It allows us to identify any self-sabotaging behaviors or limiting beliefs that hinder our relationships. Engaging in practices like journaling, therapy, or meditation can facilitate self-reflection and help us make conscious choices that are aligned with our true selves.

Creating a Supportive Community:

Finding support in a community of like-minded individuals is essential when navigating the challenges of modern relationships. Surrounding ourselves with people who share our values, offer encouragement, and provide constructive advice can empower us to make healthier choices and maintain our emotional well-being. Whether it's through friends, support groups, or online communities, building a support network can provide validation, understanding, and inspiration along our journey.

By embracing principles such as emotional intelligence, mindful technology usage, patience, acceptance, self-reflection, and creating a supportive community, we can gradually transform our relationship experiences. Through conscious efforts and a commitment to personal growth we can break free from the dating nightmare and forge meaningful connections based on authenticity, respect, and shared values.

Remember, change starts from within, and by applying the principles provided, you can create a love life that is aligned with your true desires and brings you joy, fulfillment, and genuine connection. It won't happen overnight, but with a collective commitment to change and a willingness to challenge the status quo, we can create a future where the question "When" will it be over? transforms into "When" did we start living our best lives?"

~FREEDOM

Here's a reminder, you have the choice, ability and the freedom to walk away from toxic situations. You don't have to succumb to the pressures of this WTF relationship culture. You have the power to define your own path, to break free from the confines of societal expectations, and to create a love life that aligns with your authentic self.

Now, with new sensibilities and overarching self-awareness, you can continue a journey of self-discovery and empowerment. And as you navigate the chapters of the Too Cool To LOVE study guide, we are hopeful to better prepare you to face the complexities of modern relationships, challenge the so-called norms, and to forge a path that is uniquely your own.

9

SOCIAL SERPENTS:
Too Cool To Recognize Toxic Influences

In the vast realm of human connections, a silent danger lurks beneath the surface—the Social Serpent. It slithers through our lives, disguising itself as a friend, lover, family member, or acquaintance. These toxic influences, veiled in charm and deception, possess the power to inflict emotional and psychological harm. For this reason, let's explore the importance of recognizing and escaping the clutches of Social Serpents before they totally consume you with their destructive nature.

I use the term Social Serpent to trigger the severity of noxious social influences that are lurking around you and in your life as part of your social environment. As a society, we have a natural fear or disdain for Serpents and equate them to a harmful force of some sort. Social Serpents are hurtful and harmful, and you need to stay on high alert and work overtime to keep them away from you and completely out of your life.

It is paramount for you to understand that coexisting with a Social Serpent is not wise. Their venomous presence can poison your well-being, draining you of happiness, confidence, and self-worth. They manipulate, deceive, and emotionally abuse; leaving you vulnerable and stripped of your inner strength. These insidious beings infiltrate your life, entering through the crevices of your trust and leaving a trail of devastation in their wake.

So the first step in safeguarding yourself from the Social Serpent's grasp is to become aware of its presence. These pernicious influences manifest in various forms (friends, family, etc.), but their subtle signs and behaviors remain consistent. Manipulation, deceit, and emotional abuse are their weapons of choice, and they employ them with skillful precision.

The Social Serpent thrives on convoluting your thoughts in order to manipulate your emotions, and actions. They twist your perception of reality, distorting the truth to suit their agenda. They play mind games, leaving you second-guessing yourself and questioning your own judgment. They excel at exploiting your vulnerabilities, preying on your deepest insecurities to maintain control over you. Like a master illusionist, the Social Serpent weaves a web of deceit. They craft convincing facades, presenting themselves as caring and trustworthy individuals. They shower you with false affection and promises, only to betray your trust when it serves their interests. They excel at concealing their true intentions, leaving you blindsided by their hidden agenda.

Perhaps the most dangerous aspect of the Social Serpent is its ability to inflict emotional abuse. They chip away at your self-esteem, employing subtle tactics such as belittling, gaslighting, and isolating you from your support network. They exploit your vulnerabilities, leaving you feeling inadequate and dependent on their validation. Their words and actions leave scars that may take years to heal.

Let's take a brief pause to do a health check, and a quick assessment. With growth and healing in mind, this may be a good time for you to begin thinking about taking inventory of your circle of influences and making the necessary changes to distance yourself from them.

The process of separating from Social Serpents can be challenging, but it is an essential step towards creating a healthier and more fulfilling life. This process involves a deep dive into your relationships with friends, family, acquaintances, and romantic partners to identify any destructive dynamics that may be present. It requires the willingness from you to confront uncomfortable truths and make difficult decisions for the sake of your own well-being and growth.

To begin assessing the Quality of Your Connections, and objectively evaluating the quality of your relationships, ask yourself the following questions:

- Do I feel valued, respected, and supported in these relationships?

- Are these connections based on mutual trust, honesty, and reciprocity?

- Do these individuals uplift and inspire me, or do they consistently bring me down?

- Are there patterns of manipulation, deceit, or emotional abuse in any of these relationships?

Possible Red Flags:

- Individuals who drain your energy with their persistent negativity, complaints, and toxic attitudes.

- Those who use guilt, gaslighting, or emotional manipulation to control or undermine you.

- People who are consistently absent or unsupportive when you need them, only showing up when it benefits them.

- Friends or partners who have repeatedly betrayed your trust or engaged in deceitful actions.

- Relationships where there is an imbalance of giving and receiving, with you always being the one to give more.

Now that you have answered the questions of this brief assessment, did everyone make the cut? Or like most people, do you have work to do, and deletion notices to give out, announcing you are cutting ties with some of your so-called friends and other close knit relationships?

And before going much further it is important to note that Social Serpents are not confined to the realm of personal connections alone. They extend their reach into the digital world, where platforms such as social media have become breeding grounds for their influence. Like skilled predators, they exploit your vulnerabilities, prey on your insecurities, and exert your feelings to serve their own agendas. Social media influencers, with their curated images and carefully constructed narratives, can wield immense power over your thoughts, desires, and aspirations.

In the quest for validation, you can often fall victim to the seductive allure of social media. The relentless pursuit of likes, comments, and followers can become an addiction, consuming your time, energy, and self-worth. The desire for online validation can breed comparison, envy, and feelings of inadequacy, distorting your perception of reality and creating an unhealthy obsession with external validation.

Beyond the digital realm, another set of Social Serpents lurks, the enticement of wealth, fame, and fortune. Society often glorifies the pursuit of material success, equating it with happiness and fulfillment. Yet, the unbridled pursuit of these external markers can lead you down a treacherous path, where your values become distorted, and your moral compass falters.

The attraction to money, fame, and fortune can be intoxicating, blinding you to the potential pitfalls and ruinous effects they can have on your well-being. You may find yourself compromising your integrity, sacrificing your relationships, and neglecting your own happiness in the relentless pursuit of these elusive goals. The Social Serpents of wealth and fame tighten their grip daily, leaving you entangled in a web of greed, dissatisfaction, and spiritual emptiness.

Recognizing the Signs of Social Serpents:

To protect yourself from the malicious influence of Social Serpents, you must first learn to recognize their subtle signs and behaviors. Psychological manipulation, deception, and emotional abuse are used strategically to position them to prey on your vulnerabilities, exploit your fears, and undermine your self-esteem. These virulent relationships and environments erode your emotional well-being and hinder your personal growth.

In the digital realm, the signs of Social Serpents may manifest as a constant need for validation, obsessive comparison, and an unhealthy preoccupation with image and appearance. You must be vigilant in discerning the difference between genuine connections and those driven by self-interest and manipulation.

Breaking Free:

Getting Free from the Social Serpent's grip is paramount to your well-being and personal growth. Recognizing the harmful nature of these relationships and environments is the first step toward liberation. By doing so, you create space for healthier connections to thrive and cultivate an environment that nurtures your emotional well-being.

Developing self-awareness is crucial in identifying and detaching yourself from harmful influences. Reflect on your interactions and examine the dynamics of your relationships. Trust your instincts and pay attention to any red flags that arise. Establish clear boundaries that protect your emotional well-being and enforce them with unwavering resolve.

Escaping the clutches of the Social Serpent is a daunting task, and you don't have to face it alone. Do your best to establish trusted friends, family, or professionals who can provide guidance and support. Surround yourself with a network of individuals who uplift and empower you, reinforcing your worth and helping you regain your strength.

As you distance yourself from malignant influences, prioritize self-care and healing. Nurture your mind, body, and spirit through practices that bring you joy and peace. Engage in activities that promote self-reflection and personal growth. And be patient with yourself, as healing from the wounds inflicted by the Social Serpent takes time and endurance.

Learning from the Experience:

The encounter with the Social Serpent is not in vain. Use it as an opportunity for growth and learning. Reflect on the patterns and dynamics that drew you into their grasp, and explore the underlying reasons that allowed their virulent influence to take hold. By gaining insight into your vulnerabilities and triggers, you can fortify yourself against future encounters with such influences.

The journey of escaping the Social Serpent's grip is also a path of forgiveness and letting go. Forgive yourself for any naivety or mistakes made while under their influence. Release the anger, resentment, and pain they caused, understanding that holding onto these emotions only hinders your own healing. By letting go, you free yourself from their control and make space for love and positivity to enter your life.

Taking a bold stand against Social Serpents requires courage, self-awareness, and a commitment to personal growth. It begins with acknowledging the detrimental influences in your life and making a conscious decision to distance yourself from them.

As you emerge from the clutches of the Social Serpent, you will become a beacon of strength and resilience. Share your experiences and insights with others who may be trapped in similar toxic relationships. Empower them to recognize the signs, find their voice, and reclaim their power. By offering support and guidance, you become a catalyst for positive change in their lives.

Here are 10 steps to help you understand what to do to free yourself from the grips of Social Serpents.

- 1. Awareness and Reflection: Take the time to reflect on your relationships and the impact they have on your well-being. Evaluate the role of social media and external markers of success in your life. Are they empowering or enslaving you?

- 2. Setting Boundaries: Establish clear boundaries in your interactions, both online and offline. Learn to say no to harmful relationships and environments that compromise your values and emotional well-being.

- 3. Cultivating Authentic Connections: Nurture relationships that are based on mutual respect, trust, and support. Surround yourself with individuals who uplift and inspire you, fostering a positive and nurturing environment.

- 4. Digital Detox: Take regular breaks from social media and digital platforms. Engage in activities that bring you joy, fulfillment, and a sense of connection in the real world. Rediscover the beauty of face-to-face interactions and genuine human connection.

- 5. Self-Reflection and Inner Work: Engage in self-reflection and introspection to understand your own vulnerabilities, triggers, and patterns of behavior. Work on building self-esteem, self-worth, and a strong sense of identity that is not reliant on external validation.

- 6. Cultivating Inner Strength: Develop resilience and inner strength to resist the temptations of Social Serpents. Practice self-care, mindfulness, and self-compassion to nurture your emotional well-being and protect yourself from their virulent influence.

- 7. Clarifying Values and Priorities: Define your values and prioritize what truly matters to you. Let go of the societal pressures and expectations that drive you towards the pursuit of external markers of success. Focus on creating a life aligned with your genuine desires.

- 8. Seeking Support: Reach out to trusted friends, family members, or professionals for guidance and support. Surround yourself with a support system that encourages your growth, holds you accountable, and helps you navigate the challenges of breaking free from toxic influences.

- 9. Continuous Learning and Growth: Embrace a mindset of continuous learning and personal growth. Educate yourself about healthy relationships, emotional intelligence, and psychological well-being. Equip yourself with the knowledge and tools to recognize and navigate the subtle tactics of social serpents.

- 10. Gratitude and Contentment: Practice gratitude and cultivate contentment in the present moment. Appreciate the blessings and abundance in your life, focusing on what you have rather than what you lack. This mindset shift will help you resist the allure of external validation and find fulfillment within yourself.

The Social Serpent may be cunning and elusive, but you possess the power to recognize and escape its dangerous influence. By understanding the signs and behaviors of toxic relationships, you empower yourself to protect your emotional well-being. Through self-awareness, boundaries, and seeking support, you can liberate yourself from their grasp.

Remember, you are worthy of love, respect, and healthy connections.

~Embrace your newfound freedom and use it as a catalyst for personal growth and positive change. Rise above the Social Serpent's grip and create a life filled with genuine connections, self-love, and happiness.

~Trust in your instincts, believe in your worth, and embrace the freedom that awaits you. You are capable of creating a life where nefarious influences no longer hold power over you, or your happiness and well-being.

~Remember, there is transformative power in self-love, resilience, and the pursuit of healthy relationships. So continue on the path of self-discovery, empowerment, and forging a future filled with love, fulfillment, and authentic connections.

10

R.A.P.E.:
Too Cool To Fight Abuse

Relationship
Abandonment during
Persistent and
Excessive forms of abuse (mental and physical)

The title of this chapter may evoke feelings of unease, especially for those of us who have experienced or witnessed any form of physical abuse. I write these words as someone who holds deep scarring that took years of work for me to get beyond. While I won't go into my personal experiences with molestation here, I want you to know that I write these words with empathy and the hope of fostering healing and empowerment. With that in mind, I understand that there are those who will find it hard to make the connection with this chapter. Yet if you let down the guard from the knee jerk reaction to the title, you may likely find some valuable and important tools and resources to help further your recovery.

Acknowledging and addressing the emotional trauma from abuse is an arduous journey, but it is a path we must embark upon. Together, we will navigate the rough terrain and strive for victory over the mental anguish that lies dormant, and seeks to encumber our souls. My sincere intent is that this journey will lead to a profound psychological cleanse, empowering us to heal and continue to grow. By confronting both physical assault and the pain of Relationship Abandonment after Persistent and Excessive forms of abuse, we begin the process of healing and reclaiming our lives.

Abuse, in any form, is an abhorrent and terrifying act that inflicts lasting trauma. The emotional and psychological effects of relationship abuse can mirror the anguish and lasting ramifications as physical assault. The deep scars it leaves behind can be equally devastating.

In traumatic and abusive relationships, the harm inflicted on the victim can be relentless. You may find yourself subjected to actions and behaviors that go against your will and innermost desires. The manipulation and trickery in certain relationships can confuse you, causing you to accept exploitation and mistreatment.

Let's be unequivocal: relationship abuse goes both ways and can affect and debilitate men and women equally. It is essential to recognize that any relationship that leaves you constantly hurt, sore, bruised, broken, full of mistrust, empty, and in some cases, feeling worthless, is not a healthy partnership. This type of union is toxic and will never offer any reward—

ever. Despite this, you find yourself staying in this harmful place, allowing someone to manipulate your will and take up space they should not be occupying.

I implore you to step back and take a closer look at your relationship to determine if you are a victim of this type of abuse. Acknowledging and recovering from being a victim is a difficult journey. Being stripped of your pride, dignity, and sense of worth is a gut-wrenching life experience, yet breaking away from it is often not as easy as one would think.

When you are involved with a relationship abuser, you are constantly at their mercy, as if you were their prisoner, or perhaps even a slave to the destructive partnership they have promoted. The joy and brightness that once flourished within you have been stripped away. You find yourself losing control and unable to say no, trapped and unsure of how to escape the situation.

This psychological warfare has you aware of the abuse but feeling trapped, convincing yourself that you cannot or should not leave the relationship. It's like being a hostage, locked into the sickness and degradation that your partner has insidiously convinced you to endure. You give your heart, soul, mind, body, and money, only to receive nothing in return other than being the casualty of this living hurt and pain. The irony is that you may even try to accept all of this with a smile, masking (Too Cool) the anguish within.

The control mechanisms of such an abusive relationship are merciless and inhumane. And the side-effects of their lies and broken trust will erode your heart, destroying every fiber of self-love and self-esteem.

How many times have they promised not to cheat again? How many times have they hit you, only to apologize and say they're sorry? How many times have they walked away from you, only to return and wreak havoc in your life once more? How many years have you waited for their commitment, knowing deep down it will never come? And how many more times will you allow yourself to be taken advantage of in these manners of abuse?

Rape is a serious and disturbing word, I named this chapter that intentionally to underscore the deep, hurtful association with relationship abuse. I want you to feel the seriousness and severity of the cost of actions or inactions when dealing with such a person. No one deserves to be abused and left feeling empty. Hence, you must not take this lightly. It's time to stop allowing this person, or anyone to strip you of all that you are and all that you need to protect.

Many of you experience relationship abuse daily, and in many cases, you have accepted it and continue to live in a relationship with a criminal offender. It stands to reason that if you knew someone had a reprehensible record, you would not greet them with a smile and invite them into your home. So why on earth are you sharing your life with the likes of this person? They are likened to the most heinous outlaw, yet you are planning a future with them. Do you really plan to live with this relationship fugitive, on the run for the rest of your life? Do you truly believe that this is a Bonnie and Clyde story with a life of crime that ends well?

It didn't end well for Bonnie or Clyde, and I can assure you that it will not end well for you. Your accuser or abuser is using and robbing you of all the things that should matter most to you. That is why it is imperative to remove them from your life and hold them accountable by not lowering your standards to accommodate their unacceptable behavior. You must walk away or run from this imminent danger before it is too late.

And if that isn't enough to jar you, consider this. During any type of sexual connection (including physical rape), the egg and semen have a chance to meet. Spirits and souls are still transferred (wanted or not) during this experience and could produce an unwanted pregnancy. With **Relationship Abuse,** you are constantly toying with planting seeds of opportunity that are likely to birth anguish, depression, and a lackluster level of self-love or peace in your life. And if you incubate this metaphoric child, you are likely to produce a belligerent bundle of agony, which in actuality, results in an agonizing life existence.

I know this lesson is harsh and may seem a bit over the top, but I do so intentionally because I want this to knock you around with fear and anger until it sets you free. The goal is to push you to the precipice so that you can see clearly, then act on what you need to do. Your wings are still there; you just need to use them to fly away.

If you are reading this chapter and have determined that you are in any type or form of an abusive relationship, you are experiencing R.A.P.E. This insight should be enough to compel you to garner the strength you need to fight and escape. This is not an exaggeration; I have spoken to various genders who have been victims of physical rape, and most of them agree that relationship abuse has wreaked severe havoc on their lives in many of the same ways. Therefore, unwanted or unwarranted relationship abuse cannot be allowed. But unlike physical rape, you have a choice of when and how to end the crisis.

It's important to emphasize that relationship abuse is not merely a trait of being "Too Cool To LOVE." The individual who engages in such behavior has gone beyond the boundaries of what can be considered as Too Cool to LOVE, and has ventured into a realm of sickness that can lead to complete emotional and pyscological destruction.

Like any form of physical or emotional abuse, the effects can be long-lasting, perhaps even detrimental. Many victims suffer from PTSD and even contemplate suicide. The severity of relationship abuse is just as significant as any other form of abuse, and seeking help is crucial. The weight of mental anguish, coupled with a lack of control and low self-esteem, can create a dangerous molotov cocktail that must be addressed before it leads to an explosion in your life.

People may resort to drugs or alcohol as a coping mechanism for dealing with these difficult relationship realities. However, relying on mind-altering substances is not the solution, as it only provides temporary relief and can lead to dependency—a different form of abuse in itself. It's best to face the remnants of post-traumatic stress head-on, and the first step is to confront the truth.

The Truth is, you are not a victim, and you must recognize that it's time for a change, and though it won't be easy, you now have the tools and the power to take action. Remember that you are a precious gift, and you deserve respect and protection. The dominant baseline of self-acknowledgment, self-acceptance, and self-worthiness will act as a shield, preventing you from feeling weak or vulnerable to being preyed upon.

In the sections below, and in the chapters ahead, we will explore strategies that help you break free from the chains of relationship abuse, rebuild your self-esteem, and find the strength to walk away from abusive relationships. Remember, you deserve love, respect, and a relationship built on mutual trust and care.

The next three steps are action items that require your utmost attention and commitment.

The first step involves breaking soul ties—emotionally and spiritually detaching yourself from the abuser.

The second step is your affirmation, see it as your passport to freedom.

The final step is your confession, your declaration and commitment to love yourself.

Action items:

Step 1.

Find a private space where you can scream out in anguish, allowing yourself to release the pain and drama you've experienced. Scream out a series of resolute **"NO MOREs"** to firmly assert your decision to break free from this disparagement.

Please remember that these cathartic cries and surges are not meant to prolong your suffering, but rather to purge and liberate you from the grasp of the past. You are taking action to free yourself from the pain, allowing it to dissipate from your soul and release it from your life.

Please note that this may not be for everyone. If the trauma and emotional weight of your circumstances are too heavy, please seek professional help, hopefully without the use of medication. Medication only masks the symptoms and pushes them further into your being, and you deserve to get it all out and be free!

This process of depletion can be weighty and exhausting. You will have just experienced something like outpatient surgery. So, take a few minutes to calm down and recover.

Take the same slow deep breaths needed to set up the release and use those same ones to revive you. As you are inhaling, remember that you need to love yourself. Tell yourself, "I love you." As you breathe in, see yourself happy. Put a smile on your face and acknowledge that you are clear and free to not only run in life's race, but to win.

Step 2.

This second step is your confession and affirmation of change. Say the following out loud 3-5 times with a stern posture. This time there is no need to yell or scream. You are now at peace and simply need to say this with conviction.

"I confess, I was (or am) a victim of relationship abuse. But as of today, and this moment I will not accept any form of abuse, not today or any day going forward".

"I am unique, special, and beautiful, and there is only one me. Therefore, in order for me to grow and to flourish to my maximum potential, I must protect myself and the space around me".

"No matter what anyone says, I am wonderful, and I am worthy of fruitful love and immense peace in my life".

Now confidently shout out "I Mean Everything". I Love Me, and I am the most important thing on this planet.

Your Affirmation:

You are now free from any form of enslavement. Your poison-filled belly and the tainted blood that ran through your veins are now clear, and cleansed of any toxic waste. There is no more debris in your way, and there are no more chains to lock you down or hold you in place. You have cleared the landscape for your future to produce the peace and solace you deserve.

It's incredible to witness the transformation that occurs when your aura and inner spirit are clear and radiant. Embracing your individuality and learning to love and accept yourself wholeheartedly opens doors to attracting amazing and fulfilling relationships. You become self-sufficient and content on your own, and that self-assuredness becomes a magnet for positive connections.

In life, what we believe about ourselves manifests in our reality. The power of our words shapes our experiences. So, let your daily confessions be filled with positivity and self-affirmation. Repetition turns these affirmations into habits, and soon enough, you'll truly embrace the person you are and the life you lead. Take control of your feelings and thoughts, and watch as peace and confidence become your allies.

Too Cool To LOVE

Remember, a relationship is not the source designed to complete your happiness; it is meant to complement and add to the peace and fulfillment you have already acquired. As you eagerly anticipate the right partner, focus on doing the inner work. Embrace your flaws, gifts, and talents, and love every aspect of yourself. Patience is a virtue on this journey, and when you truly love and value yourself, the right person will appear at the perfect time. And from that point forward you will establish perfect peace in every relationship.

Well, congratulations are in order, kudos to you. Take a bow of relief for getting through a very tough chapter and some rough emotional terrain. I am confident that the roads ahead will be much smoother for you. And those hurtful experiences from your past relationships have undergone a transformation. But what has actually happened is, YOU have transformed and those four stark letters of your past now stand as a testament to your growth and strength. They position you as someone that has proven to be:

Resilient with a strong and unbreakable
Aptitude towards love and the
Pursuit of an
Exemplary life...

Like a skyrocket you have been propelled towards boundless opportunities in your personal, and financial relationships. Nothing and no one can hold you back now.

Too Cool To LOVE

Breaking free from relationship abuse is a process that requires courage, perseverance, and support. Remember that you deserve a healthy, loving, and respectful relationship, and taking the steps will help you regain control over your life and move towards a brighter future.

Please complete the task below:

There are 30 steps and processes that can help you to break free, and stay safe from toxic relationships. Don't shrink away, read all 30, then the task is to identify and make a list of the "top 10" that you need to focus on, and complete.

- 1. Seek Support: Reach out to friends, family, or support groups who can provide understanding, empathy, and guidance. Having a support system can help ease the emotional burden.

- 2. Safety Plan: Create a safety plan that outlines the necessary steps to leave the abusive relationship, ensuring your physical and emotional safety during and after the process.

- 3. Build Self-Esteem and Self-Love: Engage in activities that promote self-esteem and self-love. Practice self-care, set boundaries, and celebrate your achievements, no matter how small.

- 4. Break the Isolation: Abusers often isolate their victims from friends and family.

- 5. Reconnect with loved ones and build a supportive network around you.

- 6. Educate Yourself About Abuse: Understanding the dynamics of abuse can help you recognize patterns and take appropriate action.

- 7. Document the Abuse: Keep a record of abusive incidents, such as texts, emails, or pictures, as evidence if needed later.

- 8. Cut Off Contact: Once you leave the abusive relationship, cut off all contact with the abuser to protect yourself from further harm.

- 9. Obtain Legal Protection: If necessary, seek a restraining order or other legal protection against the abuser.

- 10. Rebuild Boundaries: Learn to set healthy boundaries in your relationships, ensuring you don't fall into similar patterns in the future.

- 11. Focus on Healing: Allow yourself time to heal from the trauma. Engage in activities that bring you joy and work on personal growth.

- 12. Stay Positive and Optimistic: Surround yourself with positivity and focus on a bright future. Cultivate a positive mindset that empowers you to move forward.

- 13. Forgive Yourself: Recognize that it's not your fault you were in an abusive relationship. Forgive yourself for any perceived mistakes and focus on self-compassion.

- 14. Learn to Trust Again: Healing takes time, but when you are ready, learn to trust again in healthy relationships.

- 15. Educate Others: Use your experience to educate others about the signs of abuse and the importance of breaking free from toxic relationships.

- 16. Identify Triggers and Patterns: Understand the triggers and patterns that keep you entangled in the abusive relationship. This self-awareness can help you avoid similar situations in the future.

- 17. Practice Self-Compassion: Be gentle with yourself as you navigate the healing process. Practice self-compassion and avoid self-blame for the abuse you experienced.

- 18. Explore Your Passions: Rediscover your interests and passions. Engaging in activities you love can boost your confidence and self-esteem.

- 19. Establish Financial Independence: If possible, work towards financial independence to reduce dependency on the abuser and increase your autonomy.

- 20. Set Realistic Goals: Set achievable goals for your healing journey and celebrate your progress along the way.

- 21. Practice Mindfulness and Meditation: Mindfulness and meditation can help you stay present, reduce anxiety, and promote emotional well-being.

- 22. Engage in Physical Activities: Regular exercise can improve your mood, reduce stress, and boost your self-confidence.

- 23. Write in a Journal: Express your feelings and thoughts in a journal. Writing can be therapeutic and aid in processing emotions.

- 24. Practice Assertiveness: Learn to assertively communicate your needs and boundaries in relationships.

- 25. Avoid Self-Isolation: Resist the urge to isolate yourself. Stay connected with others who can provide support and understanding.

- 26. Volunteer or Help Others: Giving back to the community can provide a sense of purpose and fulfillment.

- 27. Focus on Growth and Personal Development: Invest in your personal growth by attending workshops, reading self-help books, or taking courses.

- 28. Seek Professional Help for Trauma: If the trauma from the abuse is overwhelming, consider seeking professional therapy or counseling to process and heal from the experience.

- 29. Reclaim Your Identity: Reconnect with activities or hobbies that bring you joy and remind you of your identity outside of the abusive relationship.

- 30. Practice Emotional Detachment: Detach emotionally from the abuser to create space for healing and personal growth.

My top 10 things to focus on and steps to take:

1. _____
2. _____

Too Cool To LOVE

3. _____
4. _____
5. _____
6. _____
7. _____
8. _____
9. _____
10. _____

Break time: Before you proceed with the final strides of the *Too Cool To LOVE* study guide, take a well-deserved 10-15 minute break. Dealing with complex emotions related to abuse can deplete and exhaust you. So take a moment to rest in your reflective journey. Then soon after, celebrate your newfound freedoms and inner beauty. Perhaps it's a good time to grab a snack, or your favorite beverage and indulge in relief and relaxation.

Go to the TooCoolToLove playlist on Spotify and let the soulful sounds of Earth Wind and Fire's song "Be Ever Wonderful" soothe and uplift you. Allow this brief interlude to solidify your sense of peace and tranquility before you continue on your journey.

11

STATE OF EMERGENCY:
Too Cool To Rescue

(Tainted)

The fiery lava of pain burst up from within women's hearts like a blustering volcano.

Their tears of anger, disgust, mistrust, and pain streams down the rigid mountain side pulling with them toxic debris that flows down into the ocean, creating an unbearable stench.

This ripple of broken emotions has generated tides of anguish creating endless streams of poison and affliction.

The water here is undrinkable, unfit for anything related to love and trust to survive. This H20 cannot quench any woman's thirst or provide relief in any way.

The waters and most of the land around her are tainted.

This poem captures how I believe many women feel in today's relationship environment. This is a State of Emergency. An urgent matter where today's independent women still find themselves dealing with a labyrinth of pain and broken emotions that threaten to block or thwart the opportunity to experience or to secure a long term relationship.

This lingering underbelly of disenchantment makes it difficult for women to open up, or open to vulnerability in relation with a man. The disparity runs deep and there are many layers of fear, control mechanisms and breaches in trust that need to be peeled off before we can establish a truce, and all begin to heal.

It may be important to note that this chapter is specific to transformation. Specific to the opportunity for men to acknowledge, and right some social and historic wrongs. By taking action, It can also be an opportunity that may allow us all to remove some pressure from the center of that torrid volcano.

I am hopeful that by now you understand, this Too Cool To LOVE study guide is dedicated to calming and healing past traumas and previous relationship dysfunction. In this case, I am hoping men can help to heal and restore faith in women, which will hopefully present an opportunity for everyone to recenter, and agree on gender opportunities and gender roles that work for today and the future.

For the men that are willing to hold up and support the actions suggested in this chapter, and the Sister I'm Sorry" movement, this footnote is for you. It is my opinion that most men understand and support the necessity and the importance of the women's empowerment movement. But many of us can also admit that it has left men wondering just where to stand in the picture. At some point men deserve the opportunity to express issues, feelings and the things that dissuade them, but this is not that chapter. This chapter is dedicated to honoring, uplifting and empowering women.

For now let's venture into the overall dynamics of this State of Emergency. With things out of balance we've seen the power dynamics between genders shift, positioning some women to operate with a defensive posture. This is fervently exemplified by the artistry of Rihanna in her soul-stirring anthem video, "You Needed Me," which echoes the emotional and relationship posture of many women today. Acknowledging this stark reality might be painful, but it's a necessary step toward understanding the magnitude of the challenge before us.

Why women first:

In the fragmented landscape of modern relationships, the State of Emergency looms large, casting a shadow over the once sacred bond between men and women. The breakdown of trust, the perpetuation of toxic discrimination, and the abuse of power have contributed to this crisis, leaving us at a crossroads where healing must begin.

The journey towards healing begins with empathy. Men must actively listen to the voices of women, hear their stories, and seek to understand the struggles they face. Empathy requires us to step into their shoes, allowing men to grasp the depth of the impact of our actions on their lives. Moreover, accountability is vital in this process. As men, we must hold ourselves accountable for the harm we've caused and take intentional steps towards change. Acknowledging our mistakes and actively working towards growth and transformation can help rebuild trust and pave the way for genuine connection.

Let's all start by first acknowledging that women are not only the backbone of our societies but also the very source of life itself. Their menstrual cycles, pregnancy, and the miraculous incubation of life within their wombs are the threads that weave the tapestry of humanity. It is through the nurturing embrace of women that each and every person on this planet has found existence. Acknowledging this fundamental truth is essential. We must celebrate the contributions of women, not just in procreation but in every aspect of life. Women's intelligence, creativity, emotional depth, and resilience enrich the fabric of our society and deserve profound respect and admiration.

Along with that, women should indeed be the cornerstone of men's love, commitment, respect, and empathy. By placing women at the center of our intentions, we recognize the significance of their presence and the invaluable role they play in our lives. Valuing women as partners, equals, and co-creators of a better world is crucial for rebuilding meaningful relationships.

Initiating the healing process requires a radical change in our approach. Instead of perpetuating the cycle of pain, men must take the first step towards reconciliation, and that starts with reaching out to women first. By doing so, we demonstrate our genuine intention to mend the wounds we've caused and rebuild trust.

Reaching out to women first signifies our commitment to creating safe spaces for vulnerability and honest communication. It demonstrates our willingness to listen and learn from their experiences, fostering an environment where mutual understanding can flourish.

As we reach out to women first, we must also break free from traditional expectations of gender roles. The journey towards healing involves dismantling the harmful constructs that have constrained both men and women in limiting roles. By embracing equality and embracing diverse expressions of gender, we lay the foundation for more authentic and fulfilling relationships.

The State of Emergency we face today is a collective challenge that requires collective healing. By initiating the journey towards reconciliation with women first, we demonstrate our commitment to breaking free from harmful patterns and rebuilding relationships based on love, trust, and empathy.

Addressing the undercurrent:

The State of Emergency in today's dating culture emerges from a complex interplay of societal shifts and historical gender roles. In recent decades, we have witnessed significant progress in breaking down traditional gender norms and promoting gender equality. Despite this, the lingering effects of toxic masculinity continue to impede genuine connections between men and women, continuing the crisis of trust and vulnerability in relationships.

At the core of this crisis lies the concept of being "Too Cool To LOVE." Men, influenced by the expectations of toxic pride, attitude and behaviors, often feel pressured to suppress their emotions and maintain a detached and aloof exterior. This facade becomes a protective shield, shielding men from potential rejection or vulnerability, resulting in challenges to build meaningful connections, often leading to superficial interactions based on bravado and surface-level appearances. Consequently, emotional expression and genuine connection suffer, as men struggle to break free from the constraints of societal expectations.

The impact of toxic masculinity and objectification goes beyond individual relationships; it permeates society as a whole. In workplaces, men may feel pressured to exhibit dominance and assertiveness, which can create hostile environments for women and other marginalized genders. The perpetuation of these harmful behaviors and attitudes contributes to an imbalance of power, further exacerbating the State of Emergency in dating culture.

But let's not overlook the fact that women too face challenges within this unrelenting toxic paradigm. While women excel in leadership positions and embrace their strength, they often long for the freedom to be vulnerable and to rely on their partners for emotional support and protection. However, the current state of things perpetuates a cycle where women feel compelled to take on masculine traits to compensate for men's emotional unavailability, leaving women yearning for genuine connection and a return to their authentic feminine nature.

To be clear, and fair, the State of Emergency requires a collective effort from all genders. Men must embark on a journey of self-awareness and emotional growth, shedding the outdated ideals of machismo. This transformation begins with acknowledging and challenging the social pressures that encourage emotional suppression and detachment. Encouraging open dialogues about emotions and vulnerability allows men to form deeper connections, fostering healthier and more fulfilling relationships.

Women can play a vital role in facilitating this transformation by supporting men's emotional expression. Empathy and understanding can help create an environment where men feel safe to break free from the "Too Cool To LOVE" persona and embrace their truth within their vulnerabilities.

The State of Emergency in modern dating and relationships demands our immediate attention. By challenging the toxic behaviors that hinders emotional expression and vulnerability, we pave the way for healthier, more meaningful connections between men and women. Embracing authenticity and breaking free from the "Too Cool To LOVE" facade allows us to cultivate relationships founded on trust, mutual respect, and emotional intimacy. Together, we can dismantle harmful patterns and create a brighter, more harmonious future for all genders.

It won't be an easy road but, as men, we need to take responsibility for our actions and the impact they have on our partners and the broader society. It is time to redefine masculinity and champion empathy, compassion, and respect. This transformation is not just essential for fostering healthy relationships but also for creating a more equitable and harmonious world.

Sister I'm Sorry:

Just like Rome, our journey toward healing and rebuilding will not be accomplished in a day. It will demand time, patience, and perseverance. In this process of reshaping, I offer you this book and its methodologies as a blueprint to guide your quest for truth. It shall serve as a source of direction, motivation, and relationship advice along the way. With this in mind, let us embark on the journey to tackle a few core issues, placing various responsibilities on men as we progress.

Gentlemen, the time has come for us to reclaim the essence of manhood - one of strength, compassion, and unwavering commitment to women. Together, we can redefine the dynamics of relationships, and in doing so, we redefine our very existence as human beings, bound by the thread of love and understanding.

The journey is just beginning, but with each step we take, we bring ourselves closer to a new reality—a reality in which men and women stand side by side, united in trust, love, and purpose. Let us take this journey together, supporting each other as we embark on the path of healing and transformation. Our future depends on it.

Men, as we move toward service, there are two items I want you to manage effectively.

The first goal is for you to take the steps to become a good man, or confirm that you are already prepared and fit to be a living example of what a good man looks like today.

In either case the checklist below will give you a snapshot of how a good man operates and how he should be postured in life, perhaps more important, how he is seen by the others in his environment. And if you are a woman reading this, they will be your guidelines to follow in order to suss things out.

Introspective Attributes of a Good Man (checklist):

- Authenticity: A good man is genuine and true to himself, unafraid to show vulnerability and emotions. He doesn't hide behind a facade but embraces his authentic self.

- Respectful: He treats everyone with respect and kindness, valuing others' opinions and perspectives without judgment.

- Empathetic: He possesses a strong sense of empathy, seeking to understand and support others, especially women, in their experiences and emotions.

- Accountability: He takes responsibility for his actions and choices, learning from his mistakes and actively working to improve and grow as a person.

- Honesty: A good man is honest and transparent in his communication, building trust through genuine and open conversations.

- Reliable: He follows through on his commitments and promises, showing consistency and dependability in his actions.

- Supportive: He is supportive of the dreams and aspirations of the women in his life, encouraging them to pursue their goals and offering a helping hand when needed.

- Active Listener: He listens attentively to others, genuinely engaging in conversations and seeking to understand their needs, desires, and concerns.

- Responsible: A responsible man takes care of his obligations, whether in his personal life, work, or relationships, demonstrating dependability and maturity.

- Emotionally Intelligent: He recognizes and understands his emotions, as well as those of others, and handles them with empathy and care.

- Non-Judgmental: He avoids making snap judgments about others, practicing compassion and understanding instead.

- Supportive of Women's Empowerment: A good man celebrates women's accomplishments and actively supports their pursuit of equality and empowerment.

- Kindness: He consistently shows kindness and consideration, creating a positive and compassionate environment for those around him.

- Communicative: He openly communicates his feelings, thoughts, and intentions, fostering a culture of trust and understanding.

- Resilient: A good man is resilient in the face of challenges, showing strength and perseverance while providing support to others during difficult times.

- Lifelong Learner: He is open to learning and self-improvement, continuously seeking ways to grow and evolve as an individual.

- Committed to Equality: He advocates for gender equality, challenging harmful stereotypes, and actively supporting the rights and empowerment of all genders.

A man with these attributes is someone who can be held in high trust and with high regard by any person (men or women) he knows or meets. A good man embodies the qualities of respect, empathy, responsibility, and authenticity, and builds meaningful and healthy relationships based on mutual understanding, trust, and genuine connection.

For the next step, and in order for you to be considered responsible enough to move toward the Sister I'm Sorry action item, you need to confirm these two things.

1. You are 100% embodying and exemplifying everything on that list.

2. You are 110% committed to standing in this gully of trauma with women, with the sole focus of helping to lift them up, and assist them with getting beyond deep emotional scars and trauma of past experiences.

If you are confident in those things, and fully committed, awesome.

Men, let's take the next transformative step and move towards uplifting and collectively support the healing of women. Let's bond together, and help to exalt them beyond their past experiences and the various levels of abuse they may have endured.

Apologies can be profound acts of compassion and solidarity. They signal a willingness to listen, learn, and hold ourselves accountable for the actions of those who have caused harm. Your apology can become a beacon of hope and support, showing these women that they are not alone, that you stand with them, and that you are committed to creating a safer and more respectful environment.

I truly hope you recognize the significance of you stepping forward with humility and empathy. In doing so, you pave the way for healing, growth, and the collective transformation of relationships between men and women. It is an opportunity to rewrite the narrative, leaving behind the scars of the past and building a future defined by respect, love, and genuine care for one another.

Remember that an apology is not about taking on someone else's guilt or shame. It is about acknowledging the pain and trauma they may have experienced and expressing sincere regret on behalf of those who have caused it. Your willingness to apologize holds immense power in fostering understanding, compassion, and ultimately, reconciliation.

Moreover, this act of apology transcends the boundaries of time and distance. It is not limited to the women directly present in your life but extends to all those who have faced harm at the hands of others. By acknowledging their pain and offering a heartfelt apology, you are acknowledging their worth and humanity.

Taking a step back to examine our actions, beliefs, and attitudes as men is a crucial aspect of personal growth. It allows you to challenge toxic behaviors and beliefs that perpetuate harm. By committing to apologize, you embrace the responsibility to break the cycle of abuse and work towards a world where all individuals are treated with dignity and respect.

As men, we have the power to redefine masculinity, not as a construct of dominance and control, but as one of compassion, vulnerability, and empathy. Apologizing and standing with women on their healing journey is a testament to the strength of character and commitment to fostering healthier relationships and communities.

Lastly, the act of apologizing to women is not one of weakness, but of strength and compassion. It acknowledges the pain caused by others and affirms your commitment to be an agent of positive change. So, thanks for stepping forward with courage, humility, and a deep sense of responsibility, for in doing so, you will play an active role in the transformation of relationships and contribute to a more loving, equitable, and understanding society.

On the other hand, Some men may think and ask, "why should I apologize? Or suggest that it does not make any sense for me to apologize to a woman I've never known, a person that I have never transgressed against in any way, shape or any form. First, I understand and acknowledge your feelings and concerns, your hesitations are valid. I will look to answer your questions as I endeavor to help you explore some reasons why this can be a powerful and meaningful step to consider.

Consider the power of collective responsibility. Even if you haven't personally harmed these women, apologizing on behalf of those who have, shows your willingness to address the broader issue of abuse and mistreatment. It's a way of standing in solidarity and promoting a culture of respect and compassion.

Apologizing can be a healing gesture, not just for others but for you as well. It communicates that you're willing to listen and understand the pain and trauma experienced by women, even if you weren't directly involved. This act of reconciliation can lead to understanding and growth for all the people connected to the process.

Think of it as breaking the cycle of harm. When you apologize, you actively challenge toxic behaviors and attitudes that perpetuate abuse. By taking responsibility for the actions of others and committing to positive change, you become part of the solution.

Remember, an apology isn't about taking on guilt or shame for something you haven't done personally. It's about acknowledging the impact others have experienced and showing compassion. Your apology can be transformative, affirming the worth and humanity of those who have been hurt.

By apologizing, you redefine masculinity in a powerful way. It's not about dominance and control but about embracing qualities like compassion, vulnerability, and empathy. These traits build deeper, more meaningful connections with others.

You're not weak for apologizing; it's a sign of strength and character. By participating in positive change and promoting healthier relationships, you contribute to creating a safer and more inclusive society for everyone.

You've got the power to make a difference. Thanks for stepping forward to consider this journey of positive change!

How this works:

Step 1: Prepare yourself:

This type of personal apology is most effective when done during a one-on-one, direct contact conversation. However, in situations where social constraints like a pandemic or long distances make a personal connection impossible, you can use various digital outlets such as FaceTime, Meet Now, or Zoom to convey your apology.

Before initiating the apology, prepare yourself for this intense and cathartic process. Understand that it may bring forth tears and emotional breakthroughs for both you and the woman receiving the apology. Choose a time and a quiet, safe space where she can absorb your words and experience the healing release she deserves.

Be mentally and emotionally ready to confront the difficult truth about the multitude of offenses and layers of betrayal and belittlement that women have endured at the hands of men. At times, you might feel a weight on your shoulders or even a hint of anger, but remember not to let those emotions cloud the process.

It's crucial to realize that while life may have moved on for many of these women, the pain they endured remains a constant companion. Few women have had anyone care enough to acknowledge their grievances, and even fewer have received a genuine apology. These strong, incredible women have navigated a world tainted by toxic masculinity, yet they have held onto their sanity. However, the memories of victimization and core hurt still linger within them. This is precisely why you are here – to make a difference.

Approach with Humility and Empathy:

As you begin the conversation, approach with humility and empathy. Acknowledge that you may never fully comprehend the depth of pain they've endured, but express your genuine desire to understand and learn. Show that you are willing to listen without judgment.

Recognize the Impact:

Take responsibility for the collective impact of men's actions and the role they have played in perpetuating a culture of harm. By acknowledging this, you demonstrate that you are not just apologizing for your personal actions but for the actions of others as well.

Express Sincere Regret:

Offer a heartfelt apology that is sincere and free of defensiveness. Avoid making excuses or minimizing the hurt caused. Instead, focus on expressing your regret for any pain, hurt, or harm that may have been inflicted on them.

Commit to Change:

Demonstrate your commitment to change by outlining the steps you will take to challenge toxic masculinity, promote empathy, and foster healthier relationships. Let them know that you are dedicated to being part of the solution and supporting their journey to healing.

Listen and Learn:

Be open to listening and learning from the woman's experiences and insights. This process is not just about your apology but about understanding the broader issues that women face and how you can actively contribute to positive change.

Offer Support:

Let her know that you are there to support her and stand in solidarity as she continues her journey towards healing and empowerment. Be a compassionate ally, willing to advocate for gender equality and dismantle harmful gender stereotypes.

Be Patient:

Healing takes time, and your apology may not immediately erase all the pain and trauma. Be patient and understand that the process is ongoing. Continue to show your support and commitment to change.

Be Accountable:

Hold yourself accountable for your words and actions moving forward. Make a conscious effort to challenge harmful behaviors and attitudes and promote respect and empathy in all your interactions.

Continue the Conversation:
Apologizing is not a one-time event; it is an ongoing commitment to growth and change. Keep the conversation alive and continue to learn from each other's experiences, fostering a culture of understanding and compassion.

Remember, while life may have moved on for many of these women, the pain they've endured remains an indelible mark on their hearts. Too often, their grievances have been ignored, and the weight of unacknowledged hurt has burdened their spirits. Genuine apologies have been a rare commodity, leaving these resilient women to bear their pain silently. Despite the challenges they've faced, they have shown remarkable strength and resilience, navigating through a world clouded by the toxic influence of masculinity.

Even as survivors, the memories of past victimization and core wounds persist, like lingering shadows that refuse to fade. They carry these burdens with them every day, influencing their self-esteem, relationships, and perception of the world. Yet, amid the struggles, they remain steadfast, unwavering in their pursuit of healing and empowerment. This is precisely why your presence and your apology matter. Your willingness to stand up and take responsibility for the collective impact of men's actions is a beacon of hope and a step towards reconciliation. By recognizing the depth of pain they've endured, you convey that their experiences are seen, heard, and acknowledged. Your sincere apology signifies that you refuse to be silent about the injustices they've faced and are committed to fostering positive change.

In this moment, you have the power to offer them something transformative – a chance to release some of the pain they've carried for far too long. Your empathy and compassion can provide a sliver of relief in their journey towards healing. By addressing the past and seeking to make amends, you become part of a powerful movement striving for a world where empathy, respect, and equality are paramount.

So, as you embark on this conversation, remember the significance of your presence and the impact of your words. Your genuine apology is not just a verbal exchange but a profound gesture that has the potential to shift the trajectory of healing and empowerment for these brave women. Let your sincerity shine through, and may your words be the catalyst that helps them reclaim their strength and find solace in the collective effort to build a more compassionate and just world.

Step 2: Ask her for permission:

Before proceeding with your apology, it is essential to seek her permission first. You are about to address deeply personal and potentially painful experiences related to abandonment, physical abuse, disappointment, heartbreak, and more – all caused by other men in her life, whether in the past or present.

Recognize that this is an incredibly private and sensitive space for her. It may be like unearthing a buried bag of afflictions, filled with emotional wounds that have been carried for years. With utmost respect and empathy, ask for her permission to enter this intimate space and offer your heartfelt apology.

Approach this request with gentleness, understanding that she may have reservations about revisiting past traumas. Allow her the space to make a choice that feels right for her. Remember, your goal is to show compassion and support, and that starts with honoring her feelings and boundaries.

One crucial point to emphasize: refrain from directly asking her to recount specific details of her past transgressions or experiences. If she chooses to unveil them voluntarily, be incredibly sensitive and attentive to the information she shares. Your role is to listen actively and offer comfort, not to pry or probe for details. In this delicate conversation, your primary role is to be an empathetic and caring listener. Give her the freedom to express herself at her own pace. She may choose to share her pain, or she may prefer to hold onto certain emotions for the time being. Allow her to guide the conversation and offer your unwavering support as she opens up.

Remember, this is a process of healing and trust-building. By asking for her permission, you demonstrate your commitment to creating a safe and respectful environment for her. Your willingness to understand her experiences without judgment speaks volumes about your sincerity and dedication to fostering a meaningful connection.

With her consent, let the conversation unfold organically. Be present and attentive, offering reassurance and empathy as she shares her feelings. And if she does decide to open up about past struggles, remember the importance of active listening – validating her emotions and experiences without attempting to fix or minimize her pain.

In this journey of healing and reconciliation, the path may be winding and unpredictable.

Trust in your intention to make a positive impact, and honor her decision to let you be a part of her healing process. Your respectful approach and heartfelt apology have the potential to be a profound turning point on her path to finding solace and empowerment. Together, you can pave the way for healing and transformation, one step at a time.

Step 3:

Once you have obtained her permission, speak from the depths of your heart and say the following in your own sincere and genuine way:

"(Name), as a woman, you are the greatest gift given to the world. I want you to know that I not only recognize your strength and resilience, but I also see your vulnerability and the beauty in your imperfections. I wholeheartedly accept you exactly as you are, and equally as important, I deeply respect and honor you for the person you are".

"And with that, I am asking you to accept my apology. Please, from the bottom of my heart, I apologize for any hurt or pain that any man before me has caused you. I apologize for any abuse or acts of transgressions against you. I deeply regret and take responsibility for any level of abandonment, disrespect, or mistreatment you have had to endure."

"I am truly sorry for each and every lie you were told, each moment your trust was shattered, and each time you were left to pick up the pieces of a broken heart. I stand in the gap against anyone who has tried to rob you of your purity, your purpose, and your self-worth."

"My sister, I am sorry. I am sorry that you had to go through any of this, and I apologize for the pain you've had to carry for so long without a proper apology."

If she allows you to, look beyond her eyes and into the depths of her soul. Let her see your sincerity and vulnerability, as you reaffirm how special and important she is to you.

Remind her that she is not defined by the actions of those who hurt her; instead, she is the true embodiment of God's best creation, deserving of love, respect, and care.

Emphasize that your intention is to provide solace and protection for her, to be a safe haven in her journey towards healing and absolution. Make it clear that you have no hidden agenda; your sole purpose is to offer genuine support and understanding.

Acknowledge that she has been carrying the weight of offenses inflicted by others, and that you stand beside her as a partner in refuge. Assure her that you will listen, learn, and strive to be a source of strength and comfort. Your aim is not to fix her pain but to be a compassionate companion on her path to reclaiming her strength and self-worth.

In this pivotal moment, let your words resonate with sincerity, empathy, and love.

This conversation is not just an exchange of apologies; it is a sacred connection between two souls, striving for healing and understanding. Together, you can forge a path towards a future defined by mutual respect, compassion, and empowerment.

What do we hope to accomplish?

The symbolic goal of the Sister I Am Sorry process is to undertake a profound act of healing and restoration. It is an opportunity for men to stand together with women, shoulder to shoulder, as they release the weight of lingering afflictions that have burdened their hearts and minds for far too long.

Through this transformative journey of apology and reconciliation, we aspire to create a powerful turning point, not only for men and women individually but for humanity as a whole. Together, we can mend our collective wounds, rewrite the narratives that have perpetuated pain and mistrust, and forge a path towards a future where trust, love, and compassion reign supreme.

This global, apologetic approach from sincere and purposeful men will set a profound tone – one of openness, compassion, and grace. It heralds the commencement of a deep cleanse and much-needed healing, transcending boundaries and cultures, and uniting us under the banner of understanding and empathy. It is a solid start to a reconciliation that has been long overdue, a step towards restoring harmony and balance to our relationships and society.

I believe that this is the divine design set forth by God. Each one of us has a unique opportunity to play our part and return to the core essence of love and truth. In doing so, we cultivate an environment of mutual respect and freedom, where every individual can thrive and flourish. When love and truth intertwine, it brings peace and balance, culminating in the wholeness and happiness we all deserve. This profound sense of fulfillment should occupy the center of life's tapestry, shaping our interactions and experiences.

Like Martin Luther King, Jr., I, too, have a dream – a dream of a world where all individuals can coexist harmoniously, where apologies and forgiveness pave the way for genuine connection and understanding. Let us embrace this dream and embark on this journey of healing together.

Once the worldwide apology has served as a balm to heal the widespread broken souls across the land, a transformation occurs. The warriors find absolution in peace, and the fiery lava of anger and resentment are extinguished. The waters of understanding and compassion clear up the debris of past grievances, and flow into clear oceans of endless opportunities. A shimmering rainbow of hope and unity adorns the crest of our collective consciousness and the piercing blue skies inspire us to soar higher than ever before.

Break time: Here is where you can take my suggestion to pause and recalibrate your thoughts, feelings and emotions with music. If allowed, it may positively impact you and help as you continue the transformative process.

Go to the TooCoolToLove playlist on Spotify and listen to "Adore You" by Harry Styles". I believe the song speaks for itself in terms of how we should view and adore each and every woman. Let's all take a moment to reflect, and let the essence of this chapter settle in.

Action item (men): It would be nice if you were brave enough to help women see the faces of such good men. If you agree, then please post a pic and tell a short story about why this is important to you, and tag us @readtoocooltolove.

12

HEALTH CHECK:
Too Cool To Diagnose It

In the dynamic journey of relationships, there comes a pivotal moment when we must pause, reflect, and perform a Health Check. Much like tending to our physical well-being through regular check-ups, we must also dedicate time to assess the vitality of our emotional connections.

This vital practice will empower you to assess the vitality of your emotional connections and ensure they align with your desired path of growth and happiness. While you may believe that being "Too Cool To LOVE" is the root of your relationship challenges, sometimes the real issue lies in being entangled in an unhealthy partnership that takes a toll on your mental, emotional, and physical well-being.

The information below is your guide towards nurturing the heart and health of your relationships, empowering you to identify and address potential harm while fostering a thriving and fulfilling bond.

Why a Health Check Matters:

Relationships, like any living entity, require care and attention to flourish. By conducting a Health Check, you gain valuable insights into the well-being of your connection and ensure it aligns with your desired path of growth and happiness.

This practice is paramount because:

a. Promotes Emotional Wellness: A Health Check enables you to identify any emotional imbalances or toxic patterns that may be affecting your mental disposition. By addressing these issues, you create space for emotional well-being to thrive.

b. Strengthens Communication: Regular assessment fosters open communication. When partners engage in honest conversations about their feelings and needs, they build a foundation of trust and intimacy.

c. Prevents Harmful Patterns: Unhealthy relationships can lead to emotional, mental, and even physical harm. By conducting a Health Check, you proactively steer clear of detrimental patterns and create a safe environment for both yourself and your partner.

d. Promotes Mutual Growth: A Health Check invites partners to reflect on their individual journeys and goals, paving the way for mutual growth and support.

Steps for a Thorough Health Check:

a. Self-Reflection: Begin by introspecting on your own emotions, thoughts, and experiences within the relationship. Be honest with yourself about your feelings and desires. What aspects of the relationship bring you joy, and which ones cause distress?

b. Assess Communication: Evaluate the quality of communication between you and your partner. Is there active listening, understanding, and empathy? Are concerns and grievances addressed openly and constructively?

c. Evaluate Trust and Respect: Trust and respect are the pillars of any healthy relationship. Consider whether these elements are present and nurtured within your connection.

d. Identify Red Flags: Watch for warning signs of toxic behavior, such as manipulation, emotional abuse, or excessive control. Acknowledge any red flags that surface during your Health Check.

e. Embrace Boundaries: Establish healthy boundaries to safeguard your emotional well-being. Boundaries are not walls; they are bridges that promote mutual respect and self-care.

f. Seek Support: Don't hesitate to seek advice from trusted friends, family, or a therapist. External perspectives can provide valuable insights and help you navigate challenges.

g. Engage in Honest Conversations: Initiate open and compassionate conversations with your partner about the relationship's state. Share your feelings and encourage them to express theirs.

h. Be Willing to Let Go: If the Health Check reveals consistent harm or irreconcilable differences, consider whether the relationship aligns with your growth and happiness. Sometimes, letting go is an act of self-love.

i. Prioritize Self-Care: Remember, your emotional well-being is of utmost importance. Engage in self-care practices to nurture your inner strength and resilience.

Cultivate a Thriving Connection:

a. Celebrate Each Other: Recognize and celebrate the unique qualities and achievements of your partner. Appreciation fosters a positive and supportive atmosphere.

b. Practice Empathy: Seek to understand your partner's perspectives and feelings, even in moments of disagreement. Empathy bridges gaps and nurtures emotional connection.

c. Communicate Love and Gratitude: Express love and gratitude regularly. Small gestures of kindness and appreciation can make a significant difference.

d. Be Open to Growth: Embrace change and personal growth. Support your partner in their journey of self-discovery and be open to evolving together.

e. Keep the Spark Alive: Prioritize moments of intimacy and connection. Engage in shared activities and keep the spark alive in your relationship.

Performing a Health Check is not a one-time event; it is an ongoing practice to nurture the heart of your relationships. Relationships, like our physical health, require conscious effort and evaluation. Identifying toxic patterns and embracing non-negotiables are essential steps towards cultivating fulfilling partnerships. Taking these steps will help you to choose connections that align with your values and contribute positively to your overall well-being. With your choices being rooted in self-respect and love, you pave the way for a future of happiness and authentic connections.

13

PURGE:

Too Cool To Delete It

Purge definition: *To delete, get rid of, remove or release. Atone for or wipe out unwanted feelings, memories, or conditions.*

Life is a precious gift that is too short to be weighed down by the shackles of broken, bruised, and sad feelings. The quest for true love can be hindered by the haunting remnants of your history or the current instability you may find yourself in. Thus, the time has come for a purge—a liberating act of atonement and release. To achieve emotional emancipation and embrace the love and peace you truly deserve, you must embark on a transformative journey to remove all disruptive and destructive elements from every facet of your life.

But, let's be careful and proceed with caution and empathy, I do not want you to rush into this sacred task. You must carefully take the time needed to uncover the core elements that have been blocking your path to peace and love—especially the love you must cultivate for yourself. In doing so, you can unearth the roots of self-deprecating behaviors and slowly begin the purge.

Purging will ultimately free you from denial and suppression because it is designed to help you confront the present pain markers head-on and refuse to let them steal light from your future. Each painful memory etched in your heart, head, and spirit must be confronted and released. Only then can you free yourself from their grip and seize the myriad of positive opportunities awaiting you.

Relationship Credit Risk:

This next section is an invitation to help you understand and establish a purging process that will lead to an increase in your psychological, behavioral and emotional stability. It will also enhance your overall life and relationship *"credit risk"* rating, known here as your *"LIFE FICO SCORE"*.

As an author and seasoned expert in banking, credit, and lending, I found myself enamored by the fascinating similarities between *personal relationships* and *traditional credit*. Drawing from my wealth of knowledge and my genuine curiosity about human connections, I couldn't resist exploring the concept of the LIFE FICO SCORE - a novel way to measure the strength of one's personal relationship credit.

In the world of finance, the FICO score has long been the gold standard for assessing an individual's creditworthiness. It comprises several core elements, each contributing a specific percentage to the overall score. And it struck me that these very elements could be compared to the dynamics of building and maintaining strong personal relationships, and understanding risk management.

As a footnote, please don't be deterred by the conventional credit insights shared in this section. At its core, Too Cool To LOVE is a relationship study guide, and its goal is to help you experience the best of love. That said, by the conclusion of this chapter, you will discover how personal relationships and traditional credit intertwine. By the time you complete this chapter, not only will you have a new construct that will lead to stronger relationships, friendships, and partnerships. You will also receive a complimentary lesson on traditional credit and how a purging method can increase your traditional FICO score, yet ultimately work the same to improve your personal LIFE FICO SCORE.

The core elements of traditional credit aka tradelines:

- A credit tradeline refers to an individual's credit account information, which is reported to credit bureaus. It includes details about credit cards, personal loans, auto loans, home loans, and other credit accounts.

- Each tradeline includes information about the creditor, the type of account (e.g., credit card, auto loan, student loans, etc.), the credit limit or loan amount, the current balance, the payment history, and the account's age.

Significance of Established Tradelines:

- Having established tradelines is crucial for building a positive credit history and a strong credit profile.

- A credit history showcases your ability to manage credit responsibly over time and is a key factor in determining your creditworthiness.

- When you apply for a major loan, such as a home mortgage or a significant non-collateral loan, lenders assess your credit history to determine your risk level as a borrower.

- Lenders typically look for a diverse mix of tradelines, including credit cards, auto loans, personal loans, student loans, and other types of credit accounts, to gauge your credit management skills.

- Having at least three established and well-managed tradelines demonstrates your financial responsibility and can improve your creditworthiness in the eyes of lenders.

Major Purchases and Tradelines:

- For significant purchases like a home or substantial non-collateral loan, lenders often require a higher level of creditworthiness due to the substantial amount of money involved.

- A positive credit history supported by multiple established tradelines (at least 3) indicates to lenders that you have a track record of responsible credit management.

- These tradelines act as a testament to your ability to make timely payments, manage debt, and handle financial commitments effectively.

- Without a sufficient number of established tradelines, you might encounter challenges in obtaining favorable loan terms or even qualifying for certain loans altogether.

Credit tradelines are a vital component of your credit history. They should not be mismanaged, over used or overlooked and play a significant role within building your overall credit worthiness.

Paying on time (payment history/late payments):

Certainly, late payments can have a significant impact on your credit score and overall credit profile. The severity of the impact depends on how late the payment is and how frequently it occurs. Here's how different levels of late payments can affect your credit:

30-Day Late Payment:

- A payment that is 30 days late is typically reported to the credit bureaus as a late payment.

- This can result in a drop in your credit score, although the decrease may not be too substantial, especially if you have a strong credit history.

- Several 30 day late payments are likey to have a significant negative impact on your credit score, as it can indicate a potential trend of financial mismanagement.

Here is a credit hack: In life, things get tight and you may not always have the money on the day your payment is due. Don't panic, you can take up to 26 days to pay a payment and avoid a 30 day late payment on your credit report. You may be charged an additional fee (a late payment fee) but it will not hit your credit report, and will not negatively impact your credit score. I suggest 26 days because depending on the month you may have 28 days, up to 31 calendar days, and trying to gauge 30 days can be tricky. So to be safe, count the days from the date of the payment due date, and do not go past 26 days from that due date. If you go past 30 days it's all downhill as further explained below.

60-Day Late Payment:

- A payment that is 60 days late is considered more severe than a 30-day late payment.

- It can lead to a further decrease in your credit score, potentially affecting your ability to qualify for new credit or loans.

- Lenders may view a 60-day late payment as a sign of financial distress or irresponsibility, which could lead to higher interest rates on new credit accounts, if obtained.

90-Day Late Payment:

- A payment that is 90 days late is even more detrimental to your credit profile.

- At this point, the account may be classified as delinquent, and the impact on your credit score can be substantial.

- A 90-day late payment can severely limit your ability to obtain new credit, and if the pattern continues, it may lead to collection efforts and a severe negative mark on your credit report.

It's important to note that the impact of a late payment can linger on your credit report for seven years, even after the account is brought current. This can affect your ability to qualify for favorable loan terms, such as lower interest rates, in the future. Additionally, the more recent the late payment, the more significant the impact on your credit score.

To mitigate the impact of late payments on your credit, it's crucial to prioritize making payments on time. If you find yourself facing financial challenges that make it difficult to meet your obligations, consider reaching out to your creditors to discuss potential solutions, such as payment plans or deferment options. Taking proactive steps to address late payments can help minimize their negative consequences on your credit health.

How to get the best FICO score (traditional credit):

Maintaining a high credit score, often measured by the FICO score, is essential for securing better loan terms, credit card offers, and overall financial stability.

Here are the overall core elements that contribute to a strong FICO score:

1. Payment History (35% of FICO score): This is the most critical factor. Making on-time payments for all your credit obligations, such as loans, credit cards, and bills, is crucial. Late payments or defaults can significantly harm your score.

2. Credit Utilization (30% of FICO score): This refers to the amount of credit you're using compared to your total available credit. It's generally recommended to keep your credit utilization below 30%. Higher credit utilization can indicate higher risk to lenders. As an example, if your overall credit limit is $10,000.00, then the goal is to borrow or use only up to $3,000.00 of it (below 30%).

3. Credit History Length (15% of FICO score): The length of your credit history matters. Generally, a longer credit history is better, as it provides a more extended track record of your financial responsibility.

4. New Credit Inquiries (10% of FICO score): Every time you apply for new credit, a hard inquiry is added to your credit report. Multiple inquiries in a short period can be seen as a sign of higher risk to lenders.

5. Credit Mix (10% of FICO score): Having a diverse mix of credit types can positively impact your score. This could include a combination of credit cards, retail accounts, installment loans, and mortgages.

To maintain a high credit score, you should:

- Pay bills on time: Late payments have a significant negative impact on your credit score. Set up reminders or automatic payments to ensure you never miss a due date.

- Keep credit utilization low: Aim to use only a small percentage of your available credit. Avoid maxing out credit cards, even if you pay them off every month.

- Avoid opening unnecessary accounts: Each new credit application results in a hard inquiry, which can temporarily lower your score. Only apply for credit when you genuinely need it.

- Build a positive credit history: The longer you responsibly manage credit, the better your credit score becomes. If you're new to credit, consider starting with a secured credit card or becoming an authorized user on someone else's account to build your history.

- Regularly check your credit report: Monitor your credit report for errors and inaccuracies. You're entitled to a free credit report from each of the three major credit bureaus (Equifax, Experian, and TransUnion) every 12 months. Correct any mistakes promptly.

Remember that building a strong credit score takes time and consistent responsible financial behavior. Be patient and diligent, and over time, your credit score should improve.

The Comparison:

How to get the best LIFE FICO SCORE):

The initial pointers provided thus far have laid the foundation for cultivating robust personal credit, and perhaps some elements of business credit, and the journey ahead will dig deeper into these insights. While my ultimate aim is to enrich your personal growth, the primary purpose of this book remains focused on guiding you towards elevating your LIFE FICO SCORE and enhancing your relationships, and / or dating experiences.

Your LIFE FICO SCORE carries profound significance for a multitude of reasons. It serves as a daily gauge of your authenticity, serenity, and equilibrium - the bedrock of overall happiness and self-assuredness. This score embodies your essence, values, and unwavering standards, signifying your unwavering commitment to your own significance.

Elevated confidence and a high life FICO score project an aura of stability.

People in your orbit will recognize your sense of completeness, viewing you as an exemplar of growth and wisdom.

Consequently, *you are uniquely positioned to be an investment-worthy partner in relationships, mirroring the principles of conventional creditworthiness.*

It's intriguing to observe that the fundamental tenets and benchmarkers of traditional and life credit are strikingly parallel. It's worth noting that global financial institutions and lenders employ FICO score metrics to gauge credibility and credit reliability. Reflecting on this, I encourage you to consider integrating a FICO score framework into your personal sphere, a matrix that can aid in managing the dynamics of the people that are the tradelines of your life.

Just as sound credit principles empower financial stability, a LIFE FICO SCORE matrix can guide your personal evolution, fostering meaningful connections and enriching your journey through its coherent structure.

The core elements of LIFE FICO SCORE:

- In the context of comparing traditional credit (FICO SCORE) with relationship credit, envision this as your "LIFE FICO SCORE". Just as tradelines play a pivotal role in traditional credit, they hold an equally crucial place in your journey of building a formidable LIFE FICO SCORE.

- Think of a tradeline as compared to having a wise mentor by your side (perhaps this book stands as one such tradeline), a steadfast friend or family member radiating equilibrium and wholeness. Another tradeline could manifest as a nurturing and secure environment fostering your growth and well-being.

Significance of Established Tradelines:

- Should you find yourself surrounded by negativity from friends, family, or any person impeding your peace or personal progress, it becomes imperative to reconsider or replace these influences with stronger, unabridged partners (tradelines). Failing to do so could hinder not only your ability to construct a successful life but also your prospects of enhancing your LIFE FICO SCORE.

- Feel free to explore additional forms of tradelines that resonate with you, but keep in mind that each tradeline must be a bedrock of unwavering support and a positive realm for your growth. Much like cultivating a robust traditional credit history, you and your life FICO score have the potential to flourish and thrive over time. Going forward, the health of your data (comprising positive experiences and wholesome relationships) significantly impacts your trajectory. To ensure a balanced mix of good experiences, you must institute stringent rules and life guidelines. These principles must champion self-assurance and authenticity. Just as a bank enforces guidelines based on specific, measurable criteria, you, too, must rigorously adhere to criteria before investing your time or energy in anyone or anything. Your unabridged criteria become your compass.

- As you diligently practice your authenticity daily, it is equally vital that those around you uphold the same standard. They should wholeheartedly comprehend and respect your core values, guidelines, and benchmarks. Your boundaries and expectations must shine with clarity, unmistakable to all, indicating what is permissible and what is not within the realm of your life.

- Acquiring the right tradelines requires dedicated effort and strategic planning. However, I assure you that as you become adept at managing them and commit to holding both yourself and others accountable to your truth, the rewards will be substantial. A history of accountability is a testament to your commitment to growth and integrity.

Major Life Commitments and Love Tradelines:

- For significant life commitments like entering into a deep and loving relationship, you should seek individuals with a higher level of personal readiness and emotional creditworthiness. Due to the substantial emotional investment involved, this is imperative.

- A positive relationship history supported by multiple established "love tradelines" (at least 3) indicates to oneself and potential partners that you have a track record of responsible and fulfilling relationships.

- These "love tradelines" act as a testament to your ability to communicate effectively, resolve conflicts, and nurture love and trust in relationships.

- Without a sufficient number of established "love tradelines," you might encounter challenges in building deep and meaningful connections or even face difficulties in sustaining long-term, loving relationships.

Much like traditional credit tradelines are crucial for financial purchases, love tradelines are vital for significant life commitments in the realm of relationships. By having at least three established and fulfilling "love tradelines," you enhance your emotional creditworthiness and increase your chances of nurturing and sustaining loving and harmonious partnership.

Paying On Time: Building Your Strong LIFE FICO SCORE.

Just as delayed payments affect your traditional credit score, delayed gestures of love, respect, value, and appreciation impact your LIFE FICO SCORE The severity of the impact escalates as the delay stretches from 30 days to 60 and 90 days, much like the consequences of late financial payments.

30, 60, and 90 Days Late in Emotional Giving:

Too Cool To LOVE

When those around you are 30 days late in expressing love, respect, value, and appreciation, it can lead to emotional uncertainty.

As the delay extends to 60 days, the impact becomes more profound, potentially causing you to question the strength of your relationships.

By the time it reaches 90 days, the emotional toll is substantial. You might feel undervalued, unloved, and disconnected from those who matter to you.

Just as traditional credit scores decline with 30, 60, and 90-day late payments, your LIFE FICO SCORE decreases as these vital emotional deposits are delayed:

- 30 Days Late: Similar to a slight drop in a credit score, you might experience a mild sense of emotional unease. The impact might be limited if your relationships have a history of being emotionally fulfilling.

- 60 Days Late: Like a more pronounced credit score decrease, you might start feeling the strain on your emotional well-being. Doubts about your relation-nships and their significance could become more pronounced.

- 90 Days Late: This stage corresponds to a substantial credit score decline. Similarly, emotional damage accumulates, potentially leading to significant strain in relationships and a negative impact on your overall emotional health.

Much like creditors assess risk with late payments, your emotional connections might perceive these delays as a lack of investment or commitment. Addressing these concerns with open communication can help prevent further damage and maintain a strong LIFE FICO SCORE.

Remember, the emotional impact of late giving can resonate long after the action. Just as financial late payments affect loan terms and interest rates, emotional late payments can affect the quality of your relationships and your overall well-being.

How to get the best LIFE FICO SCORE:

Nurturing meaningful relationships and achieving a strong LIFE FICO SCORE – the measure of your emotional well-being – requires understanding and commitment. Just as maintaining a high credit score is essential for financial stability, these core elements contribute to a robust LIFE FICO SCORE.

> 1. Relationship History (35% of LIFE FICO SCORE): This is the foundation. Maintaining consistent emotional connections, understanding, and open communication with loved ones and friends is crucial. Long

periods of emotional distance or misunderstandings can impact your overall LIFE FICO SCORE.

2. Emotional Investment (30% of LIFE FICO SCORE): Similar to credit utilization, your emotional investment ratio is significant. Striving to invest more emotional energy into meaningful relationships than you spend on developing yourself, and on self-love can lead to emotional instability. Responsible management of emotional output and utilization shows prudence, and translates into a life with balance and purpose.

3. Lifespan of Connections (15% of LIFE FICO SCORE): The duration of your relationships matters. Long-lasting, well-nurtured connections contribute positively to your LIFE FICO SCORE, showcasing your ability to maintain healthy emotional bonds.

4. New Emotional Endeavors (10% of LIFE FICO SCORE): Like credit inquiries, every time you embark on new emotional relationships or experiences, it has the potential to impact, and lower your LIFE FICO SCORE. Engaging in too many new relationships too quickly might indicate emotional instability. So use extreme caution when considering new relationship commitments, and be sure that everyone aligns with your values and goals.

5. Diversity of Emotional Bonds (10% of LIFE FICO SCORE): Similar to a traditional credit mix, having a diverse range of relationships enriches your LIFE FICO SCORE. Balancing connections with family, friends, partners, and community contributes to emotional harmony.

To maintain a high LIFE FICO SCORE, you should:

- Invest time and effort: Allocate quality time and genuine effort to nurture your relationships. Consistent emotional engagement demonstrates your commitment to the people who matter to you.

- Balance emotional investment: Strive to keep a balance between giving and receiving emotional energy. Overextending yourself emotionally can lead to burnout, just like high credit utilization can strain your financial health.

- Prioritize meaningful connections: Avoid spreading yourself thin by forming unnecessary relationships. Focusing on building strong bonds with individuals who align with your values and can enhance your overall LIFE FICO SCORE.

- Cultivate lasting connections: The longer you invest in your relationships with authenticity and empathy, the more your LIFE FICO SCORE benefits. Be patient and persistent in nurturing your connections.

- Regularly assess your emotional well-being: Reflect on your emotional health and assess the quality of your relationships. Address misunderstandings or emotional gaps promptly to maintain a strong LIFE FICO SCORE.

Remember that building a strong LIFE FICO SCORE, just like a financial credit score, takes time, dedication, and consistent efforts. By prioritizing emotional well-being and fostering meaningful connections, you can elevate your overall LIFE FICO SCORE and enjoy more fulfilling relationships.

Purging old and negative information:

Whether it's in the realm of interpersonal connections or traditional credit management, shedding old or negative data is essential. From here I will provide you with the tools and steps to Purge traditional credit issues and items. Then I will do the same as it relates to relationship credit and how to improve your LIFE FICO SCORE.

1. Managing traditional credit risk /improving your FICO score): Review Your Credit Report: Obtain a copy of your credit report from each of the major credit reporting agencies – Equifax, Experian, and

TransUnion. You're entitled to a free copy of your credit report from each agency once every 12 months. Review the reports carefully to identify any inaccuracies, errors, or outdated negative information.

2. Identify Inaccurate Items: Look for negative items that are incorrect, outdated (past the permissible reporting period), or that you believe are not your responsibility. Common negative items include late payments, collections, charge-offs, bankruptcies, and more.

3. Gather Documentation: Collect supporting documentation that proves the inaccuracy or outdated nature of the negative item. This could include payment receipts, correspondence with creditors, court documents, or any other evidence that supports your dispute.

4. Initiate a Dispute: Write a formal "dispute letter" to the credit reporting agency reporting the inaccurate information. In your letter, clearly identify the disputed item(s), explain the inaccuracy, and provide supporting documentation. You can find sample dispute letters online, and each credit reporting agency also has instructions for initiating disputes on their websites.

5. Credit Reporting Agency Investigation: The credit reporting agency is required to investigate your dispute within 30 days of receiving it. They will contact the creditor or information provider (such as a lender or collection agency) to verify the accuracy of the information. If the information cannot be verified or if it's

found to be inaccurate, the credit reporting agency must delete or correct the item.

6. Review the Results: Once the investigation is complete, the credit reporting agency will provide you with the results in writing. If the negative item was deleted or corrected, the agency will send you an updated copy of your credit report reflecting the changes.

7. Follow Up as Needed: If the credit reporting agency does not delete or correct the negative item as you believe they should, you have the right to further dispute the information. You can also contact the creditor or information provider directly to address the issue and provide them with the supporting documentation.

8. Be Persistent: The process of disputing and having negative items deleted can sometimes be time-consuming and require persistence. Keep records of all communications and documentation throughout the process.

It's important to note that accurate negative information, such as legitimate late payments or delinquencies, cannot be removed through the dispute process. Negative information that is accurate and timely will typically remain on your credit report for a specific period, such as seven years for most derogatory items.

If you're unsure about how to navigate the dispute process, you may consider seeking guidance from a credit counseling agency or a legal professional specializing in credit matters.

Managing and relationship credit risk/improving your LIFE FICO SCORE):

Your LIFE FICO SCORE isn't just a measure of your emotional well-being; it's a culmination of experiences, interactions, and feelings. Negative emotions and past traumas can linger, impacting your life and relationships just like derogatory marks impact a credit report.

Consider the weight of experiences like childhood divorce, abuse, incest, rape, or enduring hurtful words. These events can create deep emotional scars, leading to mental and emotional dysfunction. Just as lingering debts can affect your credit score, lingering negative experiences can affect your LIFE FICO SCORE.

The Purge Process:

1. Identify Negative Elements: Similar to reviewing your credit report, take time to identify negative emotions and experiences that are affecting your emotional well-being. Acknowledge them without judgment.

2. Gather Support: Just as you'd consult professionals for credit guidance, consider seeking therapy or counseling

to address your emotional traumas. Therapists and counselors can provide a safe space to discuss and heal from these experiences.

3. Challenge Negative Beliefs: Much like disputing inaccurate information, challenge negative beliefs or thoughts that have been ingrained due to past experiences. Replace them with positive affirmations and beliefs that empower you.

4. Forgiveness and Letting Go: Forgiving yourself and others is crucial. Just as errors can be corrected on a credit report, forgiving allows you to release the emotional burden and move forward.

5. Focus on Healing: Invest in activities that promote healing, growth, and positivity. Just as responsible financial behavior improves credit, practicing self-care enhances your LIFE FICO SCORE.

6. Practice Mindfulness: Similar to monitoring your credit, regularly monitor your emotional well-being. Be mindful of triggers and signs of emotional distress, and take proactive steps to address them.

7. Utilize Letters of Dispute and Deletion: Visit toocooltolove.com and access the "dispute" and "deletion" letters provided. These letters can help you notify and dispute negative actions from family members, friends, or partners that are affecting your emotional well-being. And if the dispute is not remedied, they will

be sent a letter of deletion and be completely deleted from your life account.

8. **Persistence in Healing:** Just as you would persistently dispute inaccuracies on your credit report, be persistent in your emotional healing journey. Understand that healing takes time and continuous effort.

The Transformative Power of Purging:

In the journey of understanding the parallel between traditional credit and the intricate web of relationships that shape our emotional landscape, we've explored the dynamic interplay between negative experiences and emotional well-being. As we conclude the chapter on "Purge," it's time to reflect on the profound significance of this process and unveil the true value and power it holds in elevating your LIFE FICO SCORE.

Reclaiming Emotional Freedom:

Much like the liberation experienced when inaccuracies are purged from a credit report, the process of emotional purge grants you the freedom to reclaim your emotional well-being. As you diligently confront and release the burdens of past traumas, emotional scars, and toxic relationships, you clear the path for genuine connections and positive experiences.

Unleashing Your True Potential:

Just as improving a credit score opens doors to favorable financial opportunities, purging negativity from your life uncovers your true potential. By removing the weight of emotional distress, you create space for personal growth, self-discovery, and unbridled self-expression. The power to manifest your aspirations and shape your own narrative is within your grasp.

Forging Authentic Connections:

Just as a strong credit score paves the way for beneficial financial relationships, purging toxic elements from your life fosters the cultivation of authentic connections. As you release the chain of negative experiences, you're empowered to engage in relationships that are built on trust, respect, and mutual understanding. The bonds you create become enriched with the vitality of authenticity.

Empowering Your LIFE FICO SCORE:

Purge isn't just a process; it's a profound revelation of your ability to reshape your emotional landscape. As you actively work to heal, forgive, and embrace positivity, your LIFE FICO SCORE ascends to new heights. The emotional wealth you accumulate becomes a testimony to your resilience, strength, and unwavering commitment to personal growth.

Embrace the Journey:

Embracing the Purge process requires courage, persistence, and a deep commitment to your emotional well-being. Just as one's credit score doesn't transform overnight, neither does one's LIFE FICO SCORE. The journey is transformative, marked by challenges and triumphs, setbacks and breakthroughs. But with every step, you carve a path toward a life enriched by authentic connections, emotional liberation, and a resounding sense of empowerment.

Unlock Your Possibilities:

As you navigate the complexities of purging negativity from your life, remember that you're unlocking the possibility to embrace joy, love, and fulfillment. Your LIFE FICO SCORE is a reflection of your journey – a testament to your resilience and your capacity to thrive despite adversity.

So, take the lessons from this chapter and apply them to your life with the same determination that guides you toward enhanced creditworthiness. Purge the emotional clutter, make room for positivity, and witness the remarkable transformation that occurs when you liberate yourself from the past. The power to elevate your LIFE FICO SCORE is within you, and the world is waiting to embrace your full potential, and experience your full glory.

Too Cool To LOVE

Celebrate Your Victories:

And now, it's time to celebrate. It's time to throw your hands in the air and wave them like you just don't care. The victory is yours. Go to the TooCoolToLove playlist on Spotify and listen to "All The Way Up" by DJ Khaled. Let the music wash over you as you take a few victory laps. Feel the rhythm of the song and let it resonate with the cadence of your triumphant heart.

As the beat of the music pulse through you, let it sink in that you have cleared a path to win. Remember, you are ascending, your emotional landscape is flourishing, and your life is on track to level up. With each step you take, you will unlock new potentials, build stronger connections, and shape a brighter future.

This is your moment, embrace your journey of deliverance through purging, and keep your eyes fixed on the horizon of possibilities. Keep your energy high, keep your spirit alive, and keep moving ahead with positive motion. Onward and upward, toward the light that represents you in a more radiant way. You are no longer seen as Too Cool To LOVE, you are now known as Too Valuable To LOSE.

14

NO DAYS OFF:

Too Cool To Be Vigilant

Now that you have taken the necessary steps to remove the predators and relationship falsehoods from your life, you have effectively cleaned your slate and have a clear life report. However, it's important to understand that this is just the beginning of maintaining your state of peace and freedom. Merely serving notice and purging negative influences is not enough.

In many cases, when individuals who have caused you harm are removed from your life, they don't simply disappear nor suddenly become kind-hearted. They are far from content with being ousted and could care less about the newfound freedom you've achieved. Instead, they often intensify their efforts, seeking new and alternative ways to forcefully re-enter your life to continue to inflict pain and anguish. They become determined to undermine your sense of security and breach the barriers you've built to protect your newfound peace.

You may have heard the saying, "revenge is a dish best served cold," and it holds true. However, those with cold, relentless hearts can quickly transform into heat-seeking missiles, unmercifully targeting your fortified walls and attempting to melt the steel bars you've erected. This type of cold blooded assassin will stop at nothing to break through your defenses.

So, it is essential to remain vigilant and adopt a military-like mindset, constantly on standby to diffuse any potential actions or activities from the enemy even before they draw near. You cannot afford to blink, let your guard down in any way, and you certainly cannot take a single day off. The path towards inner peace and freedom demands your commitment to continuous self-improvement, where each day becomes a testament to your unwavering resolve.

Let's take a look at the various types of adversaries that you may encounter, and need to war against:

<u>The "Imposter"</u>

Clearly you are taking the important necessary steps to clear and fortify your personal space. As you continue on this journey of self-preservation, you will inevitably encounter various types of infiltrators who pose a threat to your well-being. To better equip you to overcome them and win, I will help by identifying 3 disruptive sources that desire to break through your doors. I will give you the codes to their modus operandi, reveal their character traits and expose their psychological idiosyncrasies. This information should develop your sharpness, condition and shape your mindset, and prepare you to stand your ground daily.

The first disruptive source is the "imposter".

Imposters are individuals who deceive others by pretending to be someone they are not, all in the pursuit of gaining an advantage or exerting control. Here are a few key points for you to note and factor in.

False Identity:

Imposterism revolves around the fabrication of one's identity. They present themselves as someone they are not, making it challenging to discern their true intentions. Despite undeniable evidence pointing to their true nature, imposters possess a remarkable ability to convince you of their innocence, leading to what we refer to as "imposter blindness." It is essential to regain trust in your own perceptions and not let imposters manipulate your judgment.

Inherent Trust:

Often, we possess an inherent trust in people and tend to take their words and actions at face value. This implicit trust can make you vulnerable to imposters who exploit your willingness to believe in the authenticity of others. Being aware of this tendency and maintaining a healthy skepticism can help you avoid falling prey to their deceptive tactics.

Motivations and Backgrounds:

Imposters come from various backgrounds, and their motivations may vary. Some imposters may be seeking to escape a flawed past or reconstruct their social status. Others may be thrill-seekers who derive excitement from assuming false identities and living a life without obstacles. There are also those who resort to imposterism as a means of escaping persecution, concealing aspects of their true selves to protect their identity. Understanding these motivations can shed light on the complexities of imposterism.

Psychological Consequences:

Imposterism has far-reaching psychological consequences for both the imposter and those who fall victim to their deception. Imposters can evoke a sense of vanity and pretentiousness within you, highlighting your susceptibility to superficial impressions and the allure of titles, uniforms, or outward appearances. It is crucial to remain vigilant and not be swayed solely by external facades.

Imposter Syndrome:

It is essential to acknowledge that imposterism can also manifest within oneself. Imposter syndrome refers to the persistent fear of being exposed as a fraud, feeling unworthy of one's achievements or position. This self-doubt can lead to accepting less than you deserve from those around you. Recognizing and addressing imposter syndrome is crucial for maintaining your self-worth and ensuring that you do not undermine your own accomplishments.

In the evolving landscape of social media, out front and carefully crafted appearances can be deceiving, so it's vital to distinguish between genuine individuals and imposters. Superficial impressions based on titles, uniforms, or glamorous lifestyles should not be the sole criteria for evaluating someone's authenticity.

Protect your fortress, rid yourself of imposters without compromise. Remember, their sole purpose is to contaminate, irritate and disrupt your journey toward self-empowerment and personal growth. So remain vigilant, trust your instincts, and maintain a healthy skepticism. Your fortress is precious, and its protection is non-negotiable.

The "Intruder"

The intruder represents an emotionally unpredictable force that enters your life with malicious intent. They seek to invade your personal space, manipulate your emotions, and devalue your sense of self-worth.

Here are a few key points for you to note and factor in:

Sinister motives and emotional manipulation:

Intruders often harbor hidden agendas and display abusive behavior. They may use emotional manipulation to keep you off-balance and in a state of fear. Their intention is to assert control over you and undermine your peace of mind. By understanding their tactics, you can resist their attempts to manipulate and devalue you.

Destructive actions and isolation:

Intruders frequently resort to destructive behaviors, both physically and emotionally. They may lash out at you, even when you've done nothing wrong, as their aim is to break you down. One of their strategies is to isolate you from your support system, controlling who you interact with and distancing you from family and friends. This isolation increases their control over your life and limits your ability to seek help or escape their grasp.

Trauma bonds and guilt:

Intruders excel at creating trauma bonds, making you feel guilty and deserving of the abuse they inflict upon you. By mixing in signs of love and positive reinforcements, the intruder manipulates your emotions and makes it difficult for you to make the decision to leave the relationship. Over time, your mind and spirit wither down, and you settle in under their control, and continue to bond with them. Recognizing the reality, and the impact of trauma bonds is crucial in reclaiming your power and seeking a healthier, more loving environment.

Domestic abuse and self-love:

Intruders can be labeled as domestic abusers, as they disrupt any notion of love, especially self-love. They exploit your vulnerability and self-worth, *tearing down the foundations of your emotional well-being. They undermine your sense of self-worth and replace your keys of self-value with keys of shame and doubt. Recognizing their abusive tactics and developing an intolerance for such behavior is essential to protect yourself and cultivate a life rooted in self-love.*

Seductive manipulation:

Some intruders possess the dangerous talent of seduction, using manipulative tactics to keep you trapped in a toxic relationship. This manipulative seduction can create a web of emotional entanglement that makes it incredibly challenging to break away. It's crucial to be aware of the seductive handcuffs they use to maintain control and make informed decisions that prioritize your well-being.

Embracing intolerance for abuse:

The intruder is a relationship nemesis, seeking to bully and belittle you. Developing an intolerance for anyone who mistreats or undermines your self-worth is vital. By setting firm boundaries and refusing to accept abusive behavior, you reclaim your power and create a safe space for yourself.

Stay vigilant, prioritize your well-being, and never hesitate to seek support when dealing with intruders in your life.

The "Invited"

The invited infiltrator, also known as the subconscious invitee, highlights the importance of being cautious not to gaslight yourself or create false images of the individuals you desire to have in your life. It's crucial to differentiate between your conscious and subconscious minds, separating your conscious present desires from the unconscious ones that may have fit in your past.

It's essential to recognize that you emit signals into the universe, whether consciously or unconsciously, and these signals attract certain things, situations, and people into your life. Therefore, you must engage in a conscious and spiritual effort to avoid sending out the wrong signals that invite the uninvited. Even after purging negative influences from your life, there is still work to be done. You must be mindful not to reintroduce preconceived notions or predetermined ideologies of people into your life that are not in alignment with your values and aspirations. This requires ongoing self-reflection, maintaining a high level of integrity, self-love, and self-value, and empowering yourself to make discerning choices.

By being self-aware, mindful, and intentional, you can ensure that the people you invite into your life align with your code of conduct, and your objectives for personal growth. It's a continuous process of evaluating your desires, examining the compatibility of individuals with your authentic self, and consciously manifesting positive connections that contribute to your well-being.

With that in mind, it's important to note that this process is not about creating a rigid checklist or idealized image of a person. It's about being open to the possibilities that exist beyond your preconceived notions and allowing genuine connections to unfold naturally. It requires you to listen to our intuition, pay attention to red flags, and be willing to walk away from relationships that do not positively contribute to your life.

Remember, the power to invite or repel infiltrators lies within you. It is 100% up to you to maintain a strong sense of self, to continuously work on your personal development, and to surround yourself with people who uplift, inspire, and encourage you on your journey.

The last set of tips below are reminders, and some encouragement for you:

Unmasking the Ultimate Warrior Within:

Within you lies an untapped wellspring of strength, waiting to be unleashed. As you shed the shackles of toxic relationships and negative influences, you create space for your authentic self to emerge. By acknowledging your worth and recognizing the significance of self-value, you empower yourself to face any adversary that attempts to penetrate your newfound sanctuary.

The Power of Resilience and Steadfastness:

In this battle for personal liberation, resilience becomes your shield and steadfastness your sword. So don't be afraid to move ahead fortifying yourself against the assaults of negativity and adversity. Through unwavering commitment, self-care practices, and the cultivation of a positive mindset, you create an unassailable defense, ensuring that no external force can sway you from your path.

The Art of Setting Goals and Expectations:

As you rebuild your life mentally, emotionally and financially, it is important to set meaningful goals and establish healthy expectations. The process of envisioning your personal, financial, and relationship aspirations, will provide you with direction and motivation. By setting realistic expectations, rooted in self-respect and self-care, you ensure that your journey is guided by your own needs and desires.

Celebrating Victories and Embracing Self-Compassion:

In your pursuit of personal liberation, it is essential to celebrate your victories, no matter how small, it is important to acknowledge your progress. By fostering a supportive and nurturing relationship with yourself, you cultivate an unwavering belief in your ability to overcome obstacles and manifest your deepest desires.

In the pursuit of breaking free from the Too Cool To LOVE mindset, it is crucial to internalize the significance of "No Days Off" as more than just a catchphrase. It is a guiding principle that should permeate every aspect of your life. Every day, you must remain vigilant, committed, and active in protecting everything you have worked so hard to build.

This journey is not a linear path, but a continuous evolution of self-discovery and growth. It demands your unwavering dedication to nurturing self-love, self-esteem, joy, and happiness. It requires you to be present and engaged, willing to confront the challenges and obstacles that may arise.

Remember that your well-being is your greatest asset, and no one should have the power to undermine or diminish it. By embracing the mantra of "No Days Off," you reclaim control over your own narrative and refuse to allow toxic influences to infiltrate your life.

The process of shedding the Too Cool To LOVE mindset will undoubtedly have its ups and downs. There will be moments of doubt, moments when you stumble, and moments when you question your own strength. But in those moments, it is essential to remind yourself of the progress you have made and the person you are becoming.

As you move forward on this transformative journey, surround yourself with a support system of like-minded individuals who uplift and empower you. Take inventory of your circle and be willing to let go of those who hinder your growth or perpetuate toxic patterns.

Ultimately, the power to break free from the shackles of the Too Cool To LOVE mindset lies within you. By committing to taking "No Days Off," you affirm your worth, embrace vulnerability, and open yourself up to authentic connections and genuine love.

Too Cool To LOVE

Let the fervent message of this chapter guide you as you navigate the complexities of relationships and self-discovery. Stand strong, protect your well-being, and cultivate a life that is rooted in love, respect, and true fulfillment.

You deserve nothing less than the best from friendships and/or any external partner. *These relationships should nourish your soul, and add value to a life that is already abundantly joyous.* Remember, you are too remarkable to settle for anything less than the love you truly deserve.

15

OBEY LOVE:

Too Cool To Hear God

The key to embracing, living, and radiating love lies within comprehending its essence, holding it in reverence, and faithfully obeying its laws. Just as our devotion to the divine demands unwavering respect, so too should our approach towards love be steeped in high esteem. Love isn't merely a fleeting emotion; it's the very software that steers our familial and relational choices, a nucleus of significance that should never be trivialized, underestimated, or toyed with. Yes, love is essential, however, the fruits and benefits of love is something that has to be earned, and they can only be measured and solidified through actions and obedience.

The first proof of obeying love came from divine kindness – a kindness that created a universal harmony. "For God loved the world so much that he gave his only son, so that whoever believes in him will not perish, but have eternal life" (John

3:16). Through this act, love turned into a commitment. Love, embodied by God, showed obedience by taking the steps necessary to ensure the greater good of all, leading to a powerful sacrifice. This divine gift continues through time as our everlasting shelter, protecting us and shaping our existence. Because of this love, we all have the chance and the strength to be a symbol of potential, standing under the banner of ObeyLOVE.

For those who have strong faith in a higher power, there's a natural concern about straying from the right path. Just as there are consequences for defying divine rules, a similar unease should accompany you when you stray from the principles of love. Laws and principles are like threads woven into the fabric of our lives, both in the cosmic and earthly realms. They're important for showing respect to the Divine and to Society. Just as seeking safety from God's wrath involves following the commandments in holy texts, desiring personal freedoms—both physically and emotionally—also requires obedience. To build a strong connection with love, you need to commit to following the sacred laws that lead to self-compassion and self-love with determination. It all starts with gathering the right tools, giving yourself a little push, and embracing knowledge and acceptance. With that, the wisdom shared in these lessons should go beyond just rules and advice. They are provided in hopes that they will become the guiding light that propels you toward breaking free from the constraints of being "Too Cool To LOVE."

As this is the final chapter of the book, I am hopeful that I have added value, and that you are standing at the culmination of your journey. This is the final destination—a crossroads where your commitment is summoned forth, where the answers to What Is LOVE are locked in as part of your ethos. This is the juncture that solidifies your allegiance to yourself and thwarts you away from the Social Serpents, and no longer have you living in a WTF state of mind. Now armed with a deeper comprehension of love's essence, you are able to embark upon a voyage that is charted by the compass of your Truth. Your foundation is now fortified, a bedrock of understanding that has cast aside the trivialities of deceit, falsehoods, and heartache. The realization that Life is Too Short has settled upon you, prompting a profound shift—a resolve to stand resolute against the onslaught of R.A.P.E. In the luminous wake of your Health Check, you've sifted through the contents of your metaphorical Toolbox, discarding what no longer serves you. The Purge was unrelenting, sweeping away not only the clutter but also the allure of superficiality, epitomized by the Trophy Life phenomenon. The chains that once bound you to the constricting confines of a "Too Cool To LOVE" persona have been sundered, liberating you to move unburdened and unencumbered. No longer do you dwell in the realm of apologies and regrets. Instead, you stride boldly into the uncharted territory of a new state of mind—a realm that renders the notion of a State of Emergency obsolete. The crescendo of your choices has brought you to this precipice, where the responsibility of ObeyLOVE reigns, a mantle that carries within it a promise of commitment and empowerment. The 7 laws ahead, are more like guiding stars. They are more than mere words; they are to become the tendril of your existence. Now that you understand that there are No Days Off, you must cling to these laws as you cling to life itself, for they are your lifeline, your navigator in the tumultuous sea of existence. Engrave the 7 Laws upon your heart, inscribed as indelibly as the Ten Commandments bestowed upon Moses by God. Embrace these laws as the core of your being, make them the moral and conscious reckoning that guides your every step. Within this sacred construct, there is no room for compromise—no space for anything less than the resplendent essence of love. So let a positive life, light and understanding of love, be your only truth and Confession.

The section below will provide the 7 Laws to help you ObeyLOVE—they are the guiding principles that can illuminate your path to a life enriched by love's embrace.

Law #1: The Law of Self-Love: The Indispensable Triad - Self-Acknowledgment, Self-Acceptance, and Self-Love.

At the core of learning how to ObeyLOVE, there needs to reside a foundational truth, encapsulated by the acceptance of Self-Love. This universal principle illuminates the path towards embracing the indispensable triad of self-acknowledgment, self-acceptance, and self-love. It encourages you to prioritize your well-being, kindle a profound connection with your authentic self, that allows your inner luminosity to guide you away from a world often fixated on external offerings.

1. Recognizing Your Worthiness

The Law of Self-Love stems from the deep realization that your worthiness is inherent and undeniable. It's a declaration that you are deserving of kindness, love, and the abundant gifts life offers. This realization dismantles the self-imposed barriers that may have obscured your self-esteem, allowing the light of self-acknowledgement to brightly shine through.

2. Cultivating Inner Harmony

Self-love becomes a sanctuary of inner harmony, a haven where self-acknowledgement, self-acceptance, and self-love finds solace in you. Like a skilled conductor, you can create a symphony in your heart, and tend to the needs of your soul, and curate a balance that resonates throughout your existence.

3. Prioritizing Your Well-Being

The Law of Self-Love implores you to prioritize your well-being, unapologetically and without reservation. Recognizing that self-care isn't a mere indulgence but a profound act of self-nurturing, you invoke the power of self-acceptance. It's here that you acknowledge your physical, emotional, and mental needs, honoring yourself with the gifts of replenishment and resilience.

4. Embracing Authenticity

Self-love isn't just an oasis for your soul; it's a stage for the drama of your authenticity to unfold. Much like a well lit stage invites actors to perform without inhibition, self-love empowers you to embrace your true self without fearing judgment. This embrace of authenticity becomes a catalyst for genuine connections, urging others to do the same.

5. The Foundation of Relationships

With the Law of Self-Love, you become the cornerstone and the reason that relationships can flourish. As you extend the triad of self-love outward, you offer the overflow of your genuine affection to others. The relentless pursuit of external validation gives way to a profound sense of self-sufficiency, rendering your relationships full of mutual respect and emotional abundance.

6. Unleashing Creativity

From the heart of self-love springs forth the creative genesis. Like a dormant seed bursting into bloom, self-love unshackles your creativity from the chains of self-doubt. With a heart unburdened, you unlock the chambers of innovation, artistry, and the boundless expanse of potential residing within you.

7. Empowering Your Choices

Embracing self-love is to empower every choice you make. Your decisions, like soldiers in formation, need to align with your aspirations, and safeguard the principles of self-acceptance. As you stand resolute, you chart a course in life that harmonizes with your authentic desires.

8. Radiating Positivity

A heart drenched in self-love becomes an eternal sun, radiating positivity far and wide. Just as the sun's rays attract life's energy, self-love's aura magnetizes positivity while dispelling the darkness of negativity. You morph into a beacon of light, illuminating the paths for those fortunate enough to cross your path.

9. Cultivating Resilience

In the shelter of self-love, resilience blossoms. The heart fortified by the mix of self-acknowledgment, self-acceptance, and self-love stands resolute amidst life's thunderstorms. Challenges become mere raindrops upon your armor, and your love for yourself becomes an anchor unshaken by adversity.

10. A Journey of Unfolding

The Law of Self-Love isn't a single step but a journey of constant revelation. It's a sacred practice of nurturing your soul with compassion, fostering growth, and embracing evolution. Through peaks and valleys, victories and defeats, you honor the essence within you, embarking on a lifelong odyssey of transformation.

~Remember that, in a world that often causes you to look at things outwardly, the Law of Self-Love echoes a call to journey to look inward. By doing this, you construct a sanctuary of empowerment, authenticity, and boundless affection. This sanctuary isn't separate from the world; it's the heart from which all genuine connections emanate. As you embody the essence of self-love, you unveil the masterpiece of your existence—a testament to the extraordinary beauty nestled within your beautiful soul.

Law #2: The Law of Establishing a Life of Truth: Navigating the No Lie Zone.

The Law of Establishing a Life of Truth stands as a beacon of unwavering integrity. This guiding principle invites you to weave authenticity into the very fabric of your being, heralding truth as a keystone of your journey. As you embark on the path of love, imagine demanding a sanctuary of trust compared to the sacred No Fly Zones in the military, where truth prevails and falsehoods dare not tread.

1. The Sanctity of Truth:

Truth is the North Star guiding your actions and choices. Just as pilots heed the boundaries of a No Fly Zone, you honor the sanctity of truth, understanding that it is a non-negotiable area of your life.

2. Creating the No Lie Zone:

Much like the military enforces a No Fly Zone with unwavering commitment, you establish your personal No Lie Zone. Within this realm, deception and falsehoods find no refuge. It's a zone of unyielding authenticity where you demand and uphold truth from yourself and others.

3. Pledging to Honesty:

The Law of Establishing a Life of Truth is a solemn pledge to navigate the terrain of life with honesty as your compass. Just as aircraft avert the No Fly Zone with utmost caution, you avoid the treacherous path of deceit, valuing transparency and open-hearted communication.

4. Consequences for Deceit:

In the No Fly Zone, the military imposes severe consequences for violating its boundaries. Similarly, within the No Lie Zone, *deceit is met with serious repercussions.* By holding yourself accountable and insisting on truth, you ensure that the trust you build remains unblemished.

5. Upholding Trust:

Just as nations respect the sovereignty of a No Fly Zone, you respect the sanctity of trust. Your commitment to truth upholds your relationships, nurturing an environment where open dialogue and authenticity flourish.

6. Navigating with Clarity:

Embracing the No Lie Zone helps you to navigate through the maze of life with clarity. Like skilled pilots flying outside the No Fly Zone, you steer clear of the fog of deception, embracing the clarity that only honesty can bring.

7. A Beacon of Integrity:

By embracing the Law of Establishing a Life of Truth, you become a beacon of integrity, illuminating the path for others. Just as the No Fly Zone signifies respect for boundaries, your commitment to truth signifies your respect for the dignity of each individual.

8. Cultivating a No Lie Zone Culture:

As you fortify your No Lie Zone, you inspire others to embrace the same ethos. Together, you foster a culture where deceit withers and authenticity flourishes, nurturing relationships built on genuine connection and mutual respect.

9. Liberating Honesty:

The Law of Establishing a Life of Truth liberates you from the weight of falsehoods. In the No Lie Zone, you soar with a sense of liberation, unburdened by the shackles of deception, and embracing the liberation that only honesty can provide.

10. The Oath of Authenticity:

By establishing your No Lie Zone, you take an oath of authenticity. Much like military forces safeguard No Fly Zones, you guard the boundaries of truth, ensuring that your life is a testament to the power of honesty.

~As you embark on this journey, remember that the No Lie Zone isn't a realm of restriction but a realm of empowerment. It's where the winds of authenticity carry you to a destination of genuine connections, empowered choices, and a life untainted by deception. By anchoring your existence in truth, you navigate life's skies with a sense of purpose, authenticity, and the unshakeable commitment to uphold the Law of Establishing a Life of Truth.

Law #3: The Law of Forgive and Forget: Embracing the Liberation of Forgiveness.

Few principles hold the power to transform your emotional landscape as profoundly as the Law of Forgive and Forget. Rooted in the essence of compassion and wisdom, this guiding principle reminds you that the act of forgiveness is not just an altruistic gesture but a transformative force that redefines your own narrative.

1. The Essence of Forgiveness:

Forgiveness is the deliberate choice to release the grip of resentment and bitterness. It's a sacred act of freeing yourself from the shackles of past grievances, liberating your heart and mind to embrace healing and renewal. By forgiving, you untether yourself from the chains that anchor you to pain and suffering.

2. Healing Your Self:

Forgiveness isn't a mere favor you extend to others; it's a profound act of self-care. Holding onto grudges or anger can poison your well-being, impacting you physically, mentally, and emotionally. Embracing forgiveness allows you to reclaim your inner peace, reduce stress, and cultivate a healthier emotional state.

3. The Art of Empathy:

Forgiving others requires you to empathize with their humanity, understanding that everyone is subject to mistakes and imperfections. It's a declaration that your capacity for empathy transcends the hurt you may have endured. Through empathy, you can see the shared struggles that unite us all.

4. Unleashing Inner Freedom:

Forgiveness grants you the ultimate liberation – the freedom from being defined by past wounds. It's a conscious step towards personal empowerment. As you forgive, you shed the weight of resentment and open the door to embracing your full potential, unrestricted by the burden of past grievances.

5. Transforming Relationships:

The Law of Forgive and Forget harmonizes relationships. By forgiving, you nurture an environment of growth, understanding, and reconciliation. It bridges gaps, allows for open communication, and paves the way for renewed connections built on empathy and mutual respect.

6. Redefining Stories:

Every act of forgiveness rewrites the narrative of your life. It changes your story from one of victimhood to one of resilience and strength. Your journey is no longer marked solely by pain, but by the courage to heal and evolve.

7. The Eternal Present:

Forgiving is a way of living in the present moment. It's a declaration that the past no longer wields the power to dictate your emotions or actions. Through forgiveness, you carve a path towards a future untethered by the burdens of yesterday.

8. A Gift to Future Generations:

By embracing the Law of Forgive and Forget, you break cycles of hurt and resentment that can transcend generations. With that gift your descendants will have a legacy of empathy, compassion, and the wisdom that forgiveness cultivates.

~In a world often marred by conflict and discord, the Law of Forgive and Forget stands as a beacon of hope. It reminds you that within you lies the capacity to liberate yourself from the chains of hurt and resentment. By extending the hand of forgiveness, you pave a solid path towards healing, transformation, and the boundless possibilities of a heart unburdened by the past.

Law #4: The Law of Patience: Nurturing the Blossom of Time.

In the intricate journeys of love, patience emerges as a guiding force—an acknowledgment of love's depth and the understanding that its growth requires the nurturing touch of time. The Law of Patience invites you to embrace the art of waiting, cultivating an environment where love's delicate buds transform into radiant blossoms. Patience is the gentle whisper that reminds you that love isn't always a sprint; it's a journey that unfolds in its own rhythm.

1. Fertile Soil for Understanding:

Within the context of relationships, patience acts as fertile soil where understanding takes root and matures. It's the graceful art of allowing individuals the space to evolve, navigate life's challenges, and unveil their true selves at their own pace. By exercising patience, you honor the uniqueness of each person's growth trajectory. You refrain from hastiness, knowing that the genuine beauty lies in the authentic unfolding.

2. Nurturing Love Over Time:

In a world accustomed to instant gratification, patience stands as a potent reminder that love's fabric is woven over time. Just as a plant requires sunlight, water, and care to flourish, so does love demand the nurturing touch of patience. This law encourages you to withhold hasty conclusions and judgments, and instead, to remain open to the evolving narratives of others.

3. Embracing Love's Natural Rhythm:

Patience extends to the ebbs and flows of love itself. It's an understanding that love's intensity isn't always at its zenith; there are moments of quiet, reflection, and growth. These periods aren't a diminishment of love's power but rather a deepening of its roots. They provide an opportunity for introspection and a chance for the heart to recalibrate.

4. Illuminating Lasting Connections:

Related to love, patience serves as a bright beam of light guiding us toward lasting connections. It's the unwavering trust that love's cadence is as unique as the individuals who share it. When you master the art of patient love, you derive solace from the journey itself, valuing the incremental steps that forge a shared horizon. By nurturing patience, you cultivate a love that's profound, enduring, and perpetually blossoming—an ode to the gentle embrace of time.

5. Respecting Growth's Tempo:

Much like a gardener tending to a delicate seedling, patience involves respecting the tempo of growth. Just as you wouldn't yank a sprout from the earth to speed its growth, you grant love the time it needs to develop into its fullest expression. By doing so, you honor the inherent wisdom of love's gradual metamorphosis.

6. Savoring Each Moment:

The Law of Patience invites you to savor each moment within the journey of love. It encourages you to cherish the subtle shifts, the transformative pauses, and the evolving emotions. As you embrace each phase with patience, you find joy in the present, letting go of the compulsion to rush towards an uncertain destination.

7. Fostering Deep Bonds:

Patience is the very foundation of forging deep bonds. Just as a blacksmith tempers metal with patience to create enduring strength, your patience tempers your connections, making them resilient and profound. The bonds woven through the threads of patience are unbreakable, because their strength is fortified by the trust that time provides.

8. Embracing Unpredictability:

The Law of Patience teaches us to embrace the unpredictability of love's journey. Just as a river follows its meandering course, love may take unexpected twists and turns. With patience as your compass, you navigate these twists with grace, knowing that the journey's unfolding holds its own magic.

~Ultimately, the Law of Patience leads us to honor the concept of divine timing. Just as a flower unfurls its petals according to nature's rhythm, love's blossoming also follows a divine plan. By cultivating patience, you align yourself with this rhythm, allowing love's petals to unfurl at the perfect moment, revealing their breathtaking beauty.

Law #5: The Law of Boundless Generosity: The Value of Giving Love Unconditionally.

Too Cool To LOVE

Within the symphony of love, emerges a profound principle—the Law of Boundless Generosity. This law encapsulates love's inherent paradox—where giving multiplies the love within. It beckons you to be a bearer of love, embracing the alchemical art of giving, sharing, and teaching without attaching strings or expecting returns.

1. Custodian of Love's Treasure Chest:

Embracing this law is akin to being a custodian of a treasure chest brimming with love's riches. It encourages you to unfurl your heart and release love into every encounter, every gesture, and every connection. Just as a river flows ceaselessly, you become a conduit, allowing love to cascade freely into the lives of others, unburdened by the weight of recognition or reciprocation.

2. Love's Magic of Multiplication:

This principle acknowledges that love's true magic lies in its multiplication through sharing. By practicing boundless generosity, you wield the power to create profound connections. Your gift of love becomes an elixir that heals, uplifts, and enriches, leaving an indelible mark on those fortunate enough to cross your path.

3. The Irony of Unconditional Giving:

Ironically, love's potency amplifies when given unconditionally. By releasing expectations, you cultivate an environment for authentic connections to bloom. The Law of Boundless Generosity urges you to detach from outcomes, embody love's essence, and trust that the universe mirrors your generosity back to you in its own time and form.

4. Teaching Love, Illuminating Souls:

By sharing love's wisdom, you morph into a luminary, dispersing the light of your experiences to others. This law encourages you to incarnate the love you aspire to witness in the world. Your example inspires others to follow suit, catalyzing a ripple effect that stretches far beyond your immediate interactions.

5. Essence Expands Exponentially:

In its essence, the Law of Boundless Generosity unveils the exponential expansion of love when given unconditionally. By fostering a spirit of giving, sharing, and teaching love, you conduct a symphony of transformation. The lives you touch, seen and unseen, witness love's alchemy—an indomitable truth that the more you give, the more you receive, and the more love multiplies within and around you.

6. The Ripple Effect of Love:

The Law of Boundless Generosity initiates a ripple effect—a cascade of love radiating outward. Just as a stone's impact on water creates concentric circles that expand endlessly, your boundless generosity initiates a sequence of connections and gestures, leaving an eternal imprint of love's enduring power.

7. Transcending Transactional Love:

Transactional love is weighed with expectations; boundless generosity transcends this limitation. It's a love not bound by debts or obligations, but a selfless offering that radiates warmth and authenticity. In giving without expectation, you rekindle the essence of pure, unadulterated love.

8. Becoming Love's Conduit:

Through the Law of Boundless Generosity, you become a conduit—a bridge between hearts. As love flows freely through you, you connect souls, illuminate paths, and inspire transformations. You enable love to bridge gaps, dissolve boundaries, and mend what once seemed irreparable.

~In the grand symphony of life, the Law of Boundless Generosity plays an irreplaceable melody—a song of endless fulfillment. By giving love unconditionally, you unlock the door to a treasure trove of contentment. This law, like a masterful conductor, orchestrates a harmony of love that enriches not only the lives of others but resonates as a chorus within your own heart.

Law #6: The Law of Sovereign Guardianship: Nurturing the Sanctity Within.

In the vast realm of love, emerges a resolute principle known as the Law of Sovereign Guardianship. This law summons you to embrace a role of authority—a sentinel safeguarding the sanctity within. It implores you to stand as a protector of the cherished domains encompassing your heart, mind, and soul. Amidst a world of change and external influences, this law embodies the essence that preserving your inner sanctum is an act of profound self-love.

1. Armor of Discernment, Shield of Self-Awareness:

Embracing this law calls for donning the armor of discernment and the shield of self-awareness. It invites you to forge an unwavering presence that oversees and directs all that seeks entry into your personal realm. Similar to a guardian watching over a cherished castle, you stand as the gatekeeper of your emotional well-being, regulating the flow of thoughts, energies, and emotions desiring admittance.

2. Boundaries Shape Inner Landscape:

This principle recognizes that the boundaries you establish and the choices you make wield direct influence over your inner landscape. By acknowledging your authority to filter and curate the elements that enter your heart, mind, and soul, you cultivate an environment that nurtures your aspirations, supports your growth, and shields you from negativity's grasp.

3. Empowerment through Choice:

In wielding the mantle of sovereign guardianship, you empower yourself to utter "yes" to what elevates and "no" to what disturbs your equilibrium. This law prompts you to harness your intrinsic authority, allowing it to illuminate your interactions, relationships, and pursuits. Through alignment with this principle, you infuse your connections with purpose and intention, crafting a life that mirrors your profound values.

4. Nurturing the Sanctuary Within:

At its essence, the Law of Sovereign Guardianship beckons you to embrace your innate authority—a wisdom born from recognizing your role as steward of your well-being. As you master the art of asserting guardianship, you weave a sanctuary of love that emanates from within. This sanctuary influences every facet of your existence, shaping a symphony of self-care, self-respect, and self-love that reverberates far and wide.

5. Unwavering Sentinel of Self-Love:

You become an unwavering sentinel of self-love, standing tall amidst life's currents. This law encourages you to walk the path of self-nurturance, prioritizing your emotional landscape. By doing so, you fortify your inner walls against the winds of uncertainty and the tempests of external pressures.

6. Cultivating an Inner Stronghold:

The Law of Sovereign Guardianship teaches you to cultivate an inner stronghold—a refuge that cradles your most authentic self. This refuge becomes the vantage point from which you navigate life's challenges, shielded by the strength of your own convictions and the boundaries that you set.

7. Radiating Resilient Confidence:

As the guardian of your inner sanctum, you radiate a resilient confidence that's rooted in self-respect. Just as a lighthouse guides ships through stormy waters, your inner confidence becomes a guiding light that leads you through life's ebbs and flows.

8. The Dance of Empowerment:

Sovereign guardianship is a dance of empowerment—a choreography of setting boundaries and making choices that honor your well-being. This dance enables you to gracefully navigate relationships, interactions, and circumstances, always rooted in self-honoring decisions.

~In the grand symphony of life, the Law of Sovereign Guardianship orchestrates a melody of self-love—a song that resounds with the grace of self-respect and the harmony of self-care. By embracing this law, you become the conductor of your own inner symphony, directing the notes of love, protection, and empowerment in a crescendo that envelops your being and extends its echoes to the world around you.

Law #7: The Law of Relentless Devotion: Becoming Intoxicated by Love.

Within the vibrant tapestry of love, emerges a principle of dynamism—the Law of Relentless Devotion. This law extends an irresistible invitation, summoning you to plunge into the intoxicating currents of love. It urges you to embrace an unwavering commitment that surpasses measure, a devotion that borders on the sublime. This is the pathway to transcending the mundane and elevating your connection with love to an exalted realm.

1. Surrendering to Boundless Flow:

Embracing this law is akin to surrendering to a boundless river coursing through your very essence. It encourages the cultivation of an unyielding commitment to nurturing love in all its forms—love for self, for others, and for the world at large. Just as an addict craves their substance, this law beckons you to yearn for love with an insatiable hunger, to indulge in its beauty, and to envelop its influence as an unwavering force shaping your journey.

2. Abundant Wellspring of Love:

This principle affirms that love isn't a finite commodity, but an abundant wellspring from which you can endlessly draw. By committing yourself to this law, you liberate yourself from the constraints of scarcity. Love flows unrestrictedly through every interaction, each moment, and every thought. It's a devotion that stokes the fires of compassion, empathy, and connection, enriching your existence in immeasurable ways.

3. Infusing Intention and Purpose:

Becoming addicted to love infuses your actions with intention and purpose. The Law of Relentless Devotion beckons you to infuse even the simplest gestures with profound care and consideration. It's a call to elevate relationships from mere transactions to meaningful exchanges that carry the weight of your unwavering commitment.

4. Guiding Light of Purpose:

By embodying this law's principles, you craft a life infused with purpose and passion. Your devotion to love becomes a guiding light that steers your decisions, molds your interactions, and propels you toward realms of personal and collective transformation. In doing so, you redefine addiction as an unquenchable thirst for love's enrichment, forever elevating your journey to one of relentless devotion and boundless growth.

6. Intoxicating Symphony of Connection:

The Law of Relentless Devotion orchestrates an intoxicating symphony of connection, where every note resonates with the essence of love. This symphony invites you to dance through life with a heart full of commitment, recognizing that the more you give, the more you receive. Through devotion, you not only transform your own existence but ripple love's transformative power across the world.

6. A Tapestry Woven in Devotion:

Your life becomes a tapestry woven with threads of devotion—a masterpiece of profound connections, meaningful actions, and unwavering love. This law encourages you to imprint every encounter, every choice, and every moment with the indelible mark of your relentless commitment to love.

7. Embrace of the Exquisite:

Relentless devotion is an embrace of the exquisite—a declaration that love is worth investing in wholeheartedly. By weaving this principle into the fabric of your being, you amplify love's radiance, infusing every facet of your life with its brilliance.

8. Igniting Collective Transformation:

As you become intoxicated by love's transformative allure, you catalyze a ripple effect of collective transformation. Your commitment radiates outward, touching lives and inspiring others to embrace the intoxicating power of love's devotion.

~In the eternal dance of life, the Law of Relentless Devotion orchestrates a mesmerizing choreography of love. With every step, every gesture, and every heartbeat, you honor the symphony of connection. By living this law, you etch your story onto the annals of existence—a story of unceasing love, boundless commitment, and the intoxicating magic of relentless devotion.

The 7 LAWS OF OBEDIENCE, are not mere words, but potent keys that can unlock the doors to a life reshaped by love's sovereignty. Commit the laws to memory; etch them into your heart, and know that they hold the power to alter your existence in ways you cannot yet fathom.

Let these laws be more than knowledge; let them be your daily ritual, your steadfast companions on life's journey. Engrave them onto your soul, and upon your very being until they are as unyielding as the mountains, and as unwavering as the stars.

The thoroughfare of your life extends before you, the avenues that were once shrouded in obscurity, now bathed in the luminous glow of your newfound understanding. Today your world spins on, ever-changing, an unceasing evolution, and, armed with the knowledge covered within these lessons, you stride boldly into the horizon.

And yes, there is a voice inside of you, speaking to you. This voice may be God, or whatever higher power that you choose to follow, and if you listen closely, I believe that presence will lead you to a place of self acceptance and self-love.

Conclusion:

As we approach the final pages of this study guide, take a moment to reflect on the distance you've traveled and the wisdom you've gained. You have emerged from the depths of misrepresentation, mistrust, and abuse in relationships, armed with a toolbox of insights and strategies to navigate the path ahead.

The essence and beauty of love are no longer elusive concepts; they are the vibrant colors in the painting that frames your soul. As you turn the last page, remember that this book was not just a collection of words, but a guiding light that led you to confront fear, discard self-deprecation, and release the emotional wreckage of your past. You've learned to harness the power of purging, to liberate yourself from the clutches of toxic relationships and the shadows they cast.

I am hopeful that you see "Too Cool To LOVE" as more than a study guide; but more of a tool and a constant companion to walk with you through the process of lifting your spirit, embracing self-acceptance, and finding balance amidst life's tumultuous waves. The chapters you've read are more than ink on pages; they are stepping stones toward wisdom, transformation, and meaning.

As you stand at this crossroads, remember the lessons you've learned: the truth that resides in your heart, the multifaceted nature of love, and the strength that comes from authenticity. Each chapter was a chapter in your own narrative, a narrative that you've been empowered to shape and enrich.

The journey doesn't end here; in fact, it's just beginning. Armed with newfound insights, you are ready to write the next chapters of your life in bold strokes of truth and courage. Your destiny is one of peace, of love, and of leaving an indelible mark on the tapestry of existence. Let your legacy resonate with the world, a legacy that shouts, "I was here, and I lived a life of authenticity, of love, and of purpose."

Go forth, and embrace each moment with an open heart. Be fearless in your pursuit of meaningful connections and experiences. Embody the essence of love in all you do. As you close this book, remember that you possess the power to shape your own narrative, to infuse your life with the tinge of authenticity and to leave footprints that lead others toward their own paths of self-discovery.

Take a deep breath and big emotional bow of celebration, and go to the TooCoolToLove playlist on Spotify and listen to "I Was Here" by Beyonce.

Thank you for allowing "Too Cool To LOVE" to be a part of your journey. May your days be filled with the vibrant hues of love, and may your life be a testament to the transformative power of embracing your true self.

Too Cool To LOVE

And with all the work you have done, and will continue to do, your friends, family and loved ones will know that you are no longer Too Cool To LOVE, you're just COOL.

About Author

Terrell's journey spans decades, cultivating meaningful relationships across diverse personal and business spectrums, providing him with invaluable insight into the themes explored in "Too Cool To LOVE."

Originally from Cleveland, Ohio, Terrell shaped his early perspectives amid the city's vibrant street life. Departing Kent State University to pursue a music career, he made a pit stop in Austin, Texas, before establishing roots in Los Angeles, California, in 1990.

Transitioning from an aspiring artist to a top record executive, Terrell collaborated with major talents, including Jermaine Stewart, Madonna, Beyoncé, Hillary Duff, Usher, and more. In 2001, the industry shift prompted by Napster's impact saw

Terrell seamlessly pivot from the music business to a 20-year career as a bank executive, retiring in 2021.

Terrell's diverse experiences—spanning urban street life, the entertainment industry, corporate business acumen—combined with a deep understanding of today's dating culture uniquely equip him for this moment.

Passionate about providing meaningful resources that empower individuals, Terrell previously contributed to the acclaimed documentary "Sister I'm Sorry" and shared his wisdom in front of millions on the Oprah Winfrey show.

Terrell's new business ventures and ongoing philanthropic projects reflect his profound commitment to making a positive community impact. Follow his journey at iMeLife.com and @iamterrellmaclin.

As an author, Terrell aims to guide readers toward a prosperous life filled with self-love, self-acceptance, and self-value.

Best regards,

Too Cool To LOVE

My notes & journal:

Too Cool To LOVE

My notes & journal:

_____
_____
_____
_____
_____
_____
_____
_____
_____
_____
_____
_____
_____
_____
_____
_____
_____
_____
_____
_____
_____
_____
_____
_____
_____
_____
_____
_____
_____
_____
_____

Too Cool To LOVE

Too Cool To LOVE

My notes & journal:

Too Cool To LOVE

My notes & journal:

___

Too Cool To LOVE

Too Cool To LOVE

My notes & journal:

Too Cool To LOVE

Too Cool To LOVE

My notes & journal:

Too Cool To LOVE

Too Cool To LOVE

My notes & journal:

Too Cool To LOVE

My notes & journal:

Too Cool To LOVE

My notes & journal:

Too Cool To LOVE

Too Cool To LOVE

My notes & journal:

Too Cool To LOVE

My notes & journal:

Too Cool To LOVE

www.ingramcontent.com/pod-product-compliance
Lightning Source LLC
Chambersburg PA
CBHW071853090426
42811CB00004B/585